SUCCEED IN...

Maths

A comprehensive guide to understanding
the principles of mathematics.

Ages 11 – 14 years

Barbara Davis

ARCTURUS

ARCTURUS

This edition published in 2014 for Index Books

Copyright © 2002 Arcturus Publishing Limited
26/27 Bickels Yard, 151–153 Bermondsey Street,
London SE1 3HA

ISBN: 978-1-84193-093-0
CH000725UK
Supplier 03, Date 1213, Print run 3047

Printed in China

CONTENTS

INTRODUCTION

Succeed in Maths is both a guide and exercise book for children and parents who want to improve their knowledge and skills in mathematics.

By the end of this book, students will be able to handle algebra, simultaneous equations and geometry, understand some of the more complicated theories such as Pythagoras' theorem, and be familiar with formulæ, such as the formula used to calculate the circumference of a circle.

This book looks carefully at all the topics apporopriate for 11–14 year olds and takes account of all levels of ability. *Succeed in Maths* is laid out in a clear, concise way, with a new subject on each page. Each of these topics is explained in great detail with easy-to-follow, step-by-step instructions to help your child understand the principles and methods needed to solve the problems. On each facing page are exercises to test your child's understanding of the topics.

The book has been designed so that many of the answers and workings out can be written directly on to the pages. However, some of the answers will require graphs and other diagrams to be drawn, so ensure that your child has a working notebook for this purpose. Some of the sections will also require the use of a ruler, compass, protractor and a calculator. The answers are at the back of the book, but encourage your child not to look them up until he or she has finished each exercise.

By the time your child has finished all the exercises in this book, you should find that their understanding, speed and accuracy in even the most difficult of mathematical topics has improved immensely.

NUMBERS AND ALGEBRA

In olden times the Romans used a cumbersome number system based on letters and this made calculations slow. Our present number system uses nine digits and zero. This allows us scope to calculate complicated sums quite easily. The key to the system is the place value of a digit, i.e. the position of a number indicates its value. In the number 14372, the 2 represents two units, the 7, seven tens, the 3, three hundreds, the 4, four thousands and the 1, one ten thousand.

This can be set out as follows:

Tth	Th	H	T	U
1	4	3	7	2

It is necessary to be able to state spoken or written words as numbers. For example, twenty thousand, five hundred and fourteen = 20,514

It is also necessary to be able to write numbers as words.
For example, 45,103 = forty-five thousand, one hundred and three.

ADDING AND SUBTRACTING

When adding or subtracting it is important that numbers are put in their correct places.

SUM 1   142 + 2536

METHOD

Th	H	T	U
	1	4	2
+ 2	5	3	6
2	6	7	8

Step 1 Set out the sum according to place value, with units below units, tens below tens and hundreds below hundreds as shown. Then add up the columns.

ANSWER   **2678**

SUM 2   2536 − 142

METHOD

Th	H	T	U
2	5^4	^{13}	6
−	1	4	2
2	3	9	4

Step 1 Set out the sum according to place value.
Step 2 Now take away: Start with the units column – $6 - 2 = 4$.
Step 3 Move to the tens column – this requires the loan of 1 from the hundreds column. Now $13 - 4 = 9$.
Step 4 In the hundreds column, $4 - 1 = 3$.
Step 5 There is nothing in the thousands column to take away, so put in 2.

ANSWER   **2394**

Write in FIGURES:

a) three thousand, one hundred and twenty-nine = [ ]

b) thirty-three thousand, two hundred and four = [ ]

c) seventy-eight thousand and twenty-five = [ ]

d) sixty thousand, two hundred and two = [ ]

e) ninety thousand = [ ]

Write in WORDS:

f) 3721 = ...

g) 76214 = ...

h) 80157 = ...

i) 67002 = ...

j) 60100 = ...

ADD:

k)
```
    1   4   2   1
+       2   0   6
  _____
```

l)
```
        7   3   5   4
+   2   8   0   0   1
  _____
```

m)   207 + 30126   = [ ]

n)   65742 + 7631   = [ ]

o)   273 + 3641 + 27001   = [ ]

SUBTRACT:

p)
```
  2   6   3   1   2
-     5   2   0   1
  _____
```

q)
```
  3   6   7   4
-     2   4   5
  _____
```

r)
```
  4   3   9   2   4
-     5   6   0   4
  _____
```

s)   63721 – 52531   = [ ]

2. MULTIPLICATION

As our number system has a base of ten, multiplying and dividing by powers of ten is simply done.

TO MULTIPLY BY POWERS OF 10

If you multiply a whole number by 10 then all the digits move one place to the left. If it is multiplied by 100 or 1000, they move two or three places to the left.

For example,

278 x 10   **= 2780**   (Because you are multiplying by 10, these figures have moved one place to the left and a zero has been added to the end.)

963 x 100   **= 96300**   (Because you are multiplying by 100, these figures have moved two places to the left and two zeros have been added to the end.)

427 x 1000   **= 427000**   (Because you are multiplying by 1000, these figures have moved three places to the left and three zeros have been added to the end.)

TO MULTIPLY BY MULTIPLES OF 10

To multiply a whole number by 20 or 30, you can multiply by 2 or 3 etc, and shift the numbers of the answer one place (or two or three places in the case of 200, 300 or 2,000, 3,000) to the left.

SUM 1   **123 x 20**

METHOD

H	T	U
1	2	3
x		2
2	4	6

Step 1 Imagine you are multiplying by 2.
Step 2 Lay out the sum according to place value and multiply by 2 (2 x 3 = 6, 2 x 2 = 4, 2 x 1 = 2).
Step 3 Because you are actually multiplying by 20, shift the numbers one place to the left and add a zero.

ANSWER   **2460**

SUM 2   **312 x 300**   **= 93600**   (Because you are multiplying by 300, the figures have moved two places to the left and two zeros have been added to the end.)

SUM 3   **231 x 4000**   **= 924000**   (Because you are multiplying by 4000, the figures have moved three places to the left and three zeros have been added to the end.)

Multiply the following by the POWERS OF TEN:

a) 326 x 10 = [   ]

b) 25 x 10 = [   ]

c) 4237 x 100 = [   ]

d) 274 x 100 = [   ]

e) 27 x 1000 = [   ]

f) 62 x 1000 = [   ]

Multiply the following by the MULTIPLES OF TEN:

g) 321 x 30 = [   ]

h) 154 x 20 = [   ]

i) 231 x 300 = [   ]

j) 372 x 400 = [   ]

k) 171 x 3000 = [   ]

l) 224 x 4000 = [   ]

TO DIVIDE BY POWERS OF 10

If you divide a whole number by 10 all the digits move one place to the right. If it is divided by 100 or 1000 they move two or three places to the right.

For example,
278 ÷ 10 = 27.8

(Because you are dividing by 10, the figures have moved one place to the right and a decimal point is added.)

963 ÷ 100 = 9.63

(Because you are dividing by 100, the figures have moved two places to the right and a decimal point is added.)

TO DIVIDE BY MULTIPLES OF 10

To divide by 20 or 30 you can score off the last digit making it a remainder and divide by 2 or 3.

SUM 1   2480 ÷ 20

METHOD
$$20 \overline{\begin{array}{cccc} \textbf{Th} & \textbf{H} & \textbf{T} & \textbf{U} \\ 2 & 4 & 8 & 0 \\ \hline 1 & 2 & 4 & r0 \end{array}}$$

Step 1 Lay out the sum according to place value.
Step 2 Instead of dividing by 20, score off the last digit and divide by 2. 2 goes into 2 once, so put a 1 below the 2; 2 goes into 4 twice, so put a 2 below the 4; 2 goes into 8 four times, so put a 4 below the 8. The remainder is 0.

ANSWER   **124**

SUM 2   425 ÷ 30

METHOD
$$30 \overline{\begin{array}{ccc} \textbf{H} & \textbf{T} & \textbf{U} \\ 4 & {}^{1}2 & 5 \\ \hline 1 & 4 & r5 \end{array}}$$

Step 1 Lay out the sum according to place value.
Step 2 Instead of dividing by 30, score off the last digit and divide by 3. 3 goes into 4 once, remainder 1, so put a 1 below the four and carry the remaining 1 to the tens column. This is now 12; 3 goes into 12 four times, so put a 4 below the 12. You have scored off the last digit (5) so this can't be divided into. Therefore 5 is the remainder.

ANSWER   **14 r5**

If there is a remainder from the tens as well as the units, the tens digit goes in front of the units as a remainder.

SUM 3   445 ÷ 30

METHOD
$$30 \overline{\begin{array}{ccc} \textbf{H} & \textbf{T} & \textbf{U} \\ 4 & {}^{1}4 & {}^{2}5 \\ \hline 1 & 4 & r25 \end{array}}$$

Step 1 Lay out the sum according to place value.
Step 2 As before, score off the last digits and divide as above. When you get to the second 4, you will notice that there is a 2 left over. Note however, that this is not a unit but represents 2 tens, as it is from the tens column. This should be placed in front of the 5 in the units column. These two digits (25) are the remainder.

ANSWER   **14 r25**

Divide the following by the POWERS OF TEN:

a) 236 ÷ 10   = [＿＿＿＿]   **b)** 25 ÷ 10   = [＿＿＿＿]

c) 724 ÷ 100   = [＿＿＿＿]   **d)** 638 ÷ 100   = [＿＿＿＿]

e) 2734 ÷ 1000   = [＿＿＿＿]   **f)** 927 ÷ 1000   = [＿＿＿＿]

Divide the following by the MULTIPLES OF TEN:

g) 20 | 4 6 8 2 0   = [＿＿＿＿]

h) 40 | 8 4 2 4 1   = [＿＿＿＿]

i) 70 | 5 7 5 4 3   = [＿＿＿＿]

j) 30 | 9 6 3 4 1   = [＿＿＿＿]

k) 50 | 6 6 6 6 6   = [＿＿＿＿]

l) 60 | 2 4 7 9 3   = [＿＿＿＿]

m) 80 | 3 9 0 6 5   = [＿＿＿＿]

n) 90 | 7 7 7 7 2   = [＿＿＿＿]

4. LONG MULTIPLICATION

SUM 1   437 x 23

METHOD

H	T	U
4	3	7
x	2	3

Th	H	T	U
	4	3	7
x		(2)	3
1	3	1	1
		1	2

Th	H	T	U
	4	3	7
x		2	(3)
1	3	1	1
8	7	4	0
		1	

TTh	Th	H	T	U
		4	3	7
x			2	3
	1	3	1	1
+	8	7	4	0
1	0	0	5	1
	1			

ANSWER   **10051**

Step 1 First set out your work according to place value.

Step 2 Start multiplying. Begin with the units column and pretend at first that you are multiplying by 3. So multiply the 7 by 3 = 21. Put 1 in the units column and carry 2 to the tens column. Now multiply 3 x 3 = 9. Remember to add the 2 (from the units column) = 11. Put 1 in the tens column and carry 1 over to the hundreds column, 3 x 4 = 12, plus the one carried over = 13. Put the 3 in the hundreds column and the 1 in the thousands column = 1311.

Step 3 Next you multiply by 20. First put a 0 in the units column and simply multiply 437 by 2. Multiply the 7 by 2 = 14, put 4 in the tens column and carry one to the hundreds column. Now multiply 2 x 3 = 6 (plus the 1 carried over) = 7. Finally 2 x 4 = 8. Write this in the thousands column = 8740.

Step 4 Now add the columns together: 1311 + 8740 = 10051.

SUM 2   526 x 324

METHOD

			5	2	6
x			3	2	4
		2	1_1	0_2	4
	1	0	5_1	2	0
1	5	7_1	8	0	0
1	7	0	4	2	4

ANSWER   **170424**

Step 1 First multiply by 4 following the multiplication steps as above. 526 x 4 = 2104.

Step 2 Next multiply by 20 (3**2**4). So put a 0 in the units column and multiply the other digits (526) by 2, i.e. 10520.

Step 3 Next multiply by 300 (**3**24). So put a 0 in both the units and tens column and multiply the other digits by 3, i.e. 157800.

Step 4 Now add the columns together: 2104 + 10520 + 157800 = 170424.

TEACHER'S TIP

When you multiply by tens put a 0 in the units column.

a) 2   4   2
x   2   1
_____

+ _____
_____

b) 3   6   1
x   3   2
_____

+ _____
_____

c) 1   3   8
x   2   3
_____

+ _____
_____

d) 3   4   7
x   4   5
_____

+ _____
_____

e) 7   2   4
x   2   4
_____

+ _____
_____

f) 2   3   9
x   7   2
_____

+ _____
_____

g) 4   3   2
x   5   3
_____

+ _____
_____

h) 7   3   6
x   4   6
_____

+ _____
_____

i) 6   7   4
x   3   9
_____

+ _____
_____

j) 7   3   3
x   5   5
_____

+ _____
_____

k) 7   7   7
x   3   4
_____

+ _____
_____

l) 6   7   5
x   8   9
_____

+ _____
_____

5. LONG DIVISION

SUM 1   4692 ÷ 28

METHOD

	Th	H	T	U
		1	6	7 r 16
28	4	6	9	2
− 2		8	↓	↓
	1	8	9	
− 1 6		8		↓
		2	1	2
−	1	9	6	
			1	6

ANSWER   **167 r16**

Step 1 First set out your work according to place value.
Step 2 Divide 28 into 4. It won't go, so leave the thousands column of the answer blank.
Step 3 Divide 28 into 46. It goes once. Write this 1 above the 6.
Step 4 Multiply 1 by 28 = 28. Now write this under the 46.
Step 5 Subtract 28 from 46 = 18.
Step 6 Now bring down the next number from the sum – the 9 – and put it beside the 18, making 189 and start again.
Step 7 Divide 28 into 189. It goes 6 times. Write 6 in the answer above the 9.
Step 8 Multiply 6 by 28 = 168.
Step 9 Subtract 168 from 189 = 21.
Step 10 Now bring down the next number from the sum – the 2 – and put it beside the 21, making 212 and start again.
Step 11 Divide 28 into 212. It goes 7 times. Write 7 in the answer above the 2.
Step 12 Multiply 7 by 28 = 196.
Step 13 Subtract 196 from 212 = 16. There is no number to go on to. So 16 is the remainder. Write this on the answer at the end of the sum.

SUM 2   13224 ÷ 32

METHOD

	Tth	Th	H	T	U
			4	1	3 r 8
32	1	3	2	2	4
−	1	2	8	↓	↓
			4	2	
−			3	2	↓
			1	0	4
−				9	6
					8

ANSWER   **413 r8**

SHORT CUT
You may find this helpful: A small plum, originally from Damascus, is called a damson. The consonants in this word can be used as a guide in long division. **D** (divide) a**M** (multiply) **S** (subtract) o**N** (on to next number) – **DaMSoN**.

14

You can use your notebooks to work out these sums:

a) $21 \overline{\smash{)}5\ 0\ 8\ 7}$ = ☐   **g)** $39 \overline{\smash{)}2\ 6\ 2\ 9\ 9}$ = ☐

b) $32 \overline{\smash{)}4\ 1\ 5\ 6\ 7}$ = ☐   **h)** $89 \overline{\smash{)}6\ 0\ 0\ 5\ 5}$ = ☐

c) $24 \overline{\smash{)}8\ 3\ 3\ 3}$ = ☐   **i)** $28 \overline{\smash{)}9\ 3\ 3\ 3}$ = ☐

d) $28 \overline{\smash{)}4\ 7\ 5\ 0}$ = ☐   **j)** $21 \overline{\smash{)}1\ 1\ 0\ 0\ 7}$ = ☐

e) $37 \overline{\smash{)}2\ 0\ 6\ 6\ 9}$ = ☐   **k)** $32 \overline{\smash{)}2\ 0\ 0\ 7\ 5}$ = ☐

f) $48 \overline{\smash{)}6\ 0\ 1\ 6\ 6}$ = ☐   **l)** $53 \overline{\smash{)}2\ 6\ 7\ 2\ 0}$ = ☐

LOWEST COMMON MULTIPLE

The **LOWEST COMMON MULTIPLE** (LCM) of two numbers is the lowest number into which both numbers will divide. For example, the LCM of 4 and 6 is 12 (both 4 and 6 will go into 12). The LCM of 5 and 15 is 15 (both 5 and 15 will go into 15).

SUM 1 **Find the LCM of 6 and 8**

METHOD
Step 1 Find the common factor – a number that goes into both 6 and 8 = 2
Step 2 Then divide 6 by 2 = 3; and 8 by 2 = 4
Step 3 Now multiply the numbers together to find the LCM: 2 x 3 x 4 = 24

ANSWER **24**

FACTORS

A **FACTOR** is a number that divides exactly into another number. E.g. 1, 2, 3 and 6 are all factors of 6 as 1 x 2 x 3 = 6 and 1 x 6 = 6.
There is an easy way to find the factors of a number:

SUM 1 **Find the factors of 24**

METHOD
i) $24 \div 1 = 24$	$1 \times 24 = 24$
ii) $24 \div 2 = 12$	$2 \times 12 = 24$
iii) $24 \div 3 = 8$	$3 \times 8 = 24$
iv) $24 \div 4 = 6$	$4 \times 6 = 24$
v) $24 \div 5 = -$	(Put a dash if it does not divide exactly)
vi) $24 \div 6 = 4$	$6 \times 4 = 24$

Step 1 To cover all possible combinations start off with the number divided by 1.
Step 2 Then try dividing by the other numbers.

ANSWER **The factors of 24 are 1, 2, 3, 4, 6, 8, 12 and 24**

PRIME NUMBERS

A **PRIME NUMBER** is a number that has only two factors: itself and 1. The first three prime numbers are 2, 3 and 5 (1 doesn't count as it only has one factor). Prime numbers may end in 1, 3, 7 or 9.

SUM 1 **Find the prime numbers between 60 and 70**

METHOD **Step 1** Look at the numbers ending in 1, 3, 7 and 9. These are 61, 63, 67, 69
61 can only be divided by itself and 1 – it IS a prime number.
63 can be divided by 1, 7, 9 and 63 – it is NOT a prime number.
67 can only be divided by itself and 1 – it IS a prime number.
69 can be divided by many numbers – it is NOT a prime number.

ANSWER **The prime numbers between 60 and 70 are 61 and 67**

PRIME FACTORS

Sometimes you may be asked for the **PRIME FACTORS** of a large number. Simply find the factors and split these into prime numbers. For example, 72 = 12 x 6 = 2 x 6 x 2 x 3 = 2 x 2 x 3 x 2 x 3.
Therefore the prime factors of 72 are 2 x 2 x 2 x 3 x 3.

Just by looking, find the LCM (Lowest Common Multiple) of the following numbers:

a) 2, 3 = ☐   **b)** 3, 4 = ☐ **c)** 5, 2 = ☐

d) 2, 3, 4 = ☐   **e)** 6, 4 = ☐ **f)** 7, 3 = ☐

g) 4, 10 = ☐   **h)** 2, 5, 4 = ☐

Find the HCF (Highest Common Factor) of the following numbers:

i) 10, 15 = ☐   **j)** 4, 12 = ☐ **k)** 6, 15 = ☐

l) 7, 28 = ☐   **m)** 20, 32 = ☐ **n)** 30, 45 = ☐

o) 8, 60 = ☐   **p)** 63, 81 = ☐

Write down all the PRIME NUMBERS between those given below:

q) 2 and 10 ☐ ☐ ☐

r) 10 and 20 ☐ ☐ ☐ ☐

s) 40 and 55 ☐ ☐ ☐ ☐

Write down all the PRIME FACTORS of the numbers listed below:

t) 12 ....   **u)** 35 ....   **v)** 48 ....

w) 60 ....   **x)** 84 ....   **y)** 144 ....

TEACHER'S TIP
For numbers up to 120, you can simply divide by 3 or 7, to see if they are prime. For example, 63 ÷ 7 = 9 AND 69 ÷ 3 = 23.

TERMS & SYMBOLS
A **multiple** is the result of multiplying one number by another
E.g. 2 x 5 = 10. So 10 is a multiple of 2; 10 is also a multiple of 5.
The **Highest Common Factor** (HCF) of two numbers is the highest factor common to both. For example, the HCF of 10 and 25 is 5 (both 10 and 25 can be divided by 5).

To be clear about **POSITIVE** and **NEGATIVE** numbers, it is useful to draw a number line as shown below:

A number to the **right** of another one is bigger than it. For example, **6 > 3, –1 > –5**. A number to the **left** of another one is smaller, e.g **–5 < –2 and 1 < 5.**

ADDITION AND SUBTRACTION

SUM 1   2 – 5

METHOD

Step 1 Start at 0 and count forward two. From there count back five.

ANSWER   **–3**

> ### TEACHER'S TIP
> When signs are different, subtract the figures and take the sign of the larger number. For example, -5 + 2 = -3 (5 – 2 = 3 then use the sign of the 5 = -3).

Sometimes there are two signs between two numbers. Two like signs (i.e. + and + or – and –) are equal to one positive (+) sign. Two unlike signs (i.e. – and +) are equal to one negative (–) sign.

For example,
7 + (+2) = 7 + 2 = 9
7 – (–2) = 7 + 2 = 9
7 – (+2) = 7 – 2 = 5
7 + (–2) = 7 – 2 = 5

MULTIPLICATION AND DIVISION

In multiplication and division, two like signs give a positive answer; two unlike signs give a negative answer.

For example:

LIKE SIGNS	**UNLIKE SIGNS**
+3 x +4 = +12	–3 x +4 = –12
+16 ÷ +4 = +4	–16 ÷ +4 = –4
–10 x –4 = +40	+3 x –4 = –12
–16 ÷ –4 = +4	+16 ÷ –4 = –4

GREATER OR SMALLER – Add the appropriate sign, > or <, to each of the following:

a) 5 ☐ 3   **b)** –5 ☐ 3   **c)** –6 ☐ 2   **d)** 4 ☐ –2

Put these INTEGERS (whole numbers) in order (using the number line on the previous page to help at first).

e) –2, 1, –3 → ☐   **f)** 7, –3, 1, –1 → ☐

g) 4, –5, –2, 3 → ☐   **h)** –1, 6, –3, 5 → ☐

i) –1, 6, –5, 4 → ☐

ADD together or SUBTRACT the following integers:

j) 6 + 4 = ☐   **k)** 6 – 4 = ☐   **l)** 4 – 6 = ☐

m) –6 + 4 = ☐   **n)** –1 + 5 = ☐   **o)** 1 – 5 = ☐

p) 3 – 5 = ☐   **q)** –2 + 4 = ☐

MULTIPLY or DIVIDE the following integers:

r) 6 x 4 = ☐   **s)** 6 x –4 = ☐   **t)** –7 x –3 = ☐

u) –2 x 4 = ☐   **v)** –3 x –5 = ☐   **w)** 20 ÷ 5 = ☐

x) 20 ÷ –5 = ☐   **y)** –6 ÷ –3 = ☐   **z)** –36 ÷ 9 = ☐

8. INDICES OR POWERS

2^2 means 2 x 2. The small 2 is known as the index or power. 2^2 is spoken as 2 to the power of 2.

2^3 means 2 x 2 x 2. 2^3 is spoken as 2 to the power of 3.

2^4 means 2 x 2 x 2 x 2. 2^4 is spoken as 2 to the power of 4.

When **MULTIPLYING** you add the powers. For example, 3^2 x 3^3 = 3^{2+3} = 3^5 OR 3 x 3 x 3 x 3 x 3.

You can only do this if the main number is the same.

3^2 x 4^3 cannot be written as a single number in index form because the main numbers are different (3^2 x 4^3 = 3 x 3 x 4 x 4 x 4).

When **DIVIDING** you subtract the powers. For example,

$5^7 \div 5^4 = 5^{7-4} = 5^3$ OR 5 x 5 x 5.

Remember, $4^3 \div 3^2$ cannot be written as a single number in index form because the main numbers are different

$(4^3 \div 3^2 = \dfrac{4 \times 4 \times 4}{3 \times 3})$.

When **RAISING ONE POWER TO ANOTHER,** you multiply the indices.

For example, $(2^4)^3 = 2^{4 \times 3} = 2^{12}$.

The sum is saying that you need to multiply 3 lots of 2^4 together.

Write simply 2^4 x 2^4 x 2^4.

The integer always remains the same i.e. 2.

Now simply add the indices together 4 + 4 + 4 = 12.

Answer = 2^{12}.

However, it is much quicker to write $(2^4)^3$ than 2^4 x 2^4 x 2^4.

RULE:

• Anything to the power of 1 remains the same. For example $14^1 = 14$.

• 1 to any power is 1. For example, $1^2 = 1$ (1 x 1 = 1)

$1^9 = 1$ (1 x 1 x 1 x 1 x 1 x 1 x 1 x 1 x 1)

• When a power is a fraction it means the root. For example,

$9^{1/2}$ means $\sqrt{9}$ (The square root of 9 is 3 (3 x 3 = 9))

$8^{1/3}$ means $\sqrt[3]{8}$ (The cube root of 8 is 2 (2 x 2 x 2 = 8))

ESTIMATING ROOTS If you are asked to estimate the square root of (i) 40 and (ii) 90, here are a few simple steps to help you:

Step 1 Find the square roots that you know are close to these numbers.

(i) 40. The closest squares to this are $\sqrt{36}$ = 6; and $\sqrt{49}$ = 7. Therefore $\sqrt{40}$ lies between 6 and 7.

(ii) 90. The closest squares to this are $\sqrt{81}$ = 9; and $\sqrt{100}$ = 10. Therefore $\sqrt{90}$ lies between 9 and 10.

TEST 8

MULTIPLY the following indices (leave the answers in index form):

a) $2^3 \times 2^5$ = [   ]   **b)** $7^2 \times 7^3$ = [   ]

c) $2^3 \times 2^2 \times 2^4$ = [   ]   **d)** $8^4 \times 7^2$ = [   ]

DIVIDE the following:

e) $7^4 \div 7^2$ = [   ]   **f)** $6^5 \div 6^3$ = [   ]

g) $12^7 \div 12^2$ = [   ]   **h)** $9^2 \div 3^2$ = [   ]

In the following, RAISE ONE POWER TO ANOTHER:

i) $(2^2)^3$ = [   ]   **j)** $(9^5)^2$ = [   ]

Give the value of the following numbers in POWERS OF 1 AND 0:

k) 7^1 = [   ]   **l)** 7^0 = [   ]

m) 19^1 = [   ]   **n)** 25^0 = [   ]

Give the value of the following SQUARE AND CUBE ROOTS:

o) $64^{1/2}$ = [   ]   **p)** $\sqrt{49}$ = [   ]

q) $27^{1/3}$ = [   ]   **r)** $\sqrt[3]{8}$ = [   ]

Between which WHOLE NUMBERS would these answers lie?

s) $\sqrt{20}$ = [   ] [   ]   **t)** $\sqrt{12}$ = [   ] [   ]

u) $\sqrt{30}$ = [   ] [   ]   **v)** $\sqrt{55}$ = [   ] [   ]

What is the VALUE of each of the following?

w) 1^2 = [   ]   **x)** 1^{64} = [   ]

A **FRACTION** is part of something. The most common fraction is a half, which is one of two equal parts and can be written as $^1/_2$.

The top line of a fraction is called the numerator and the bottom line is called the denominator.

Look at these fractions: $^2/_4$ $^3/_6$ $^4/_8$ $^5/_{10}$

They are also equal to a half, but in their cases the 'whole' has been broken into 4, 6, 8 and 10 equal parts and 2, 3, 4 and 5 are shares.

TERMS & SYMBOLS

Improper fractions – are greater than one, with the numerator being a higher number than the denominator e.g. $^6/_5$.

Mixed numbers – a whole number with a fraction as the remainder e.g. $1^1/_5$.

EQUIVALENCES

If you wanted to make the simple fraction $^2/_3$ equivalent to one with larger digits, such as $^{10}/_{15}$, the numerator and denominator must be multiplied by the same number. For example,

$$^2/_3 = \frac{2 \times 5}{3 \times 5} = \frac{10}{15}$$ (Both are multiplied by 5.)

$$^3/_8 = {}^9/_{24} \frac{(3 \times 3)}{(8 \times 3)}$$ (Both are multiplied by 3.)

Conversely, the numerator and denominator of a fraction with large numbers may be divided by the highest common factor, HCF (page 17) to bring it to its lowest terms. This is called cancelling.

For example, to bring $^4/_{12}$ to its lowest terms.
First find the HCF = 4 (4 goes into itself once and 12 three times).

$^4/_{12}$ becomes $\dfrac{4^1}{12^3} = \dfrac{1}{3}$

IMPROPER FRACTIONS AND MIXED NUMBERS

To change an improper fraction to a mixed number and vice versa:

SUM 1   **Change $^6/_5$ to a mixed number**

METHOD $^6/_5 = 1^1/_5$

Step 1 Divide the numerator (6) by the denominator (5). It goes once. Write this 1 down as a whole number. There is one left over. This is the remainder and becomes the new numerator. Place it over the original denominator = $1^1/_5$.

SUM 2   **Change $2^3/_4$ to an improper fraction**

METHOD $2 \times 4 = 8$
$8 + 3 = 11 = {}^{11}/_4$

Step 1 Multiply the whole number (2) by the denominator (4), $2 \times 4 = 8$.
Step 2 Add the numerator (3), $8 + 3 = 11$. Now write it as an improper fraction = $^{11}/_4$.

TEST 9

Fill in the MISSING NUMBER:

a) $\dfrac{1}{5} = \dfrac{2}{\square}$

b) $\dfrac{3}{7} = \dfrac{\square}{21}$

c) $\dfrac{3}{4} = \dfrac{9}{\square}$

d) $\dfrac{2}{9} = \dfrac{\square}{27}$

e) $\dfrac{3}{8} = \dfrac{9}{\square}$

f) $\dfrac{6}{7} = \dfrac{\square}{42}$

Bring the following to their LOWEST TERMS:

g) $\dfrac{2}{8} = \square$

h) $\dfrac{3}{12} = \square$

i) $\dfrac{8}{12} = \square$

j) $\dfrac{27}{30} = \square$

k) $\dfrac{22}{55} = \square$

l) $\dfrac{35}{49} = \square$

Convert the following to MIXED NUMBERS:

m) $\dfrac{21}{8} = \square$

n) $\dfrac{17}{5} = \square$

o) $\dfrac{25}{6} = \square$

p) $\dfrac{17}{3} = \square$

q) $\dfrac{23}{4} = \square$

r) $\dfrac{34}{7} = \square$

Convert the following to IMPROPER FRACTIONS:

s) $2^1/_2 = \square$

t) $6^1/_4 = \square$

u) $5^2/_3 = \square$

v) $4^3/_8 = \square$

w) $8^7/_8 = \square$

x) $10^2/_5 = \square$

y) $3^7/_{12} = \square$

z) $7^8/_9 = \square$

TEACHER'S TIP
Cancelling means dividing the top and bottom lines by the common factor. NEVER cancel two top or bottom lines with each other.

ADDING FRACTIONS

When adding simple fractions with the same denominator, just add the numerators.

For example, $\frac{2}{9} + \frac{3}{9} = \frac{5}{9}$

In order to add fractions with different denominators, you must first change the denominators to the same number, using the LCM (see page 16), then change the numerator to balance the fraction.

SUM 1 $\frac{2}{3} + \frac{1}{9}$

METHOD $\frac{6}{9} + \frac{1}{9} = \frac{7}{9}$

Step 1 Find the LCM = 9 (3 goes into 9 three times and into itself once).This 9 becomes the new denominator. To balance the equation change the numerator by the same amount. In fraction 1 ($\frac{2}{3}$), the denominator was changed by 3 (3 into 9 = 3), so change the numerator by 3 (2 x 3 = 6). In fraction 2 ($\frac{1}{9}$) the denominator wasn't changed (9 into 9 = 1). So the numerator remains 1.
Step 2 Now add them up.

ADDING MIXED NUMBERS

When adding mixed numbers, add the whole numbers first and treat the rest as in addition of fractions (above).

SUM 1 $8\frac{1}{2} + 3\frac{1}{3}$

METHOD $11\frac{1}{2} + \frac{1}{3}$

So, $11\frac{3}{6} + \frac{2}{6} = 11\frac{5}{6}$

Step 1 Add the whole numbers (8 + 3 = 11).
Step 2 Now make the denominators the same by finding the LCM (6: 2 goes into 6 three times and 3 goes into 6 twice). Now change the numerators by the same amounts 1 x 3 and 1 x 2 (see above).
Step 3 Now turn into a mixed number (see page 22).

SUBTRACTING FRACTIONS

Exactly the same method is used for subtracting fractions.

$\frac{3}{4} - \frac{2}{5} = \frac{15}{20} - \frac{8}{20} = \frac{7}{20}$

Step 1 Find the LCM of 4 and 5 = 20. This 20 becomes the new denominator. To balance the equation change the numerator by the same amount 3 x 5 = 15 and 2 x 4 = 8.
Step 2 Now take them away.

When subtracting MIXED NUMBERS, subtract the whole numbers first and treat the rest as in subtraction of fractions (see above).

$8\frac{1}{2} - 3\frac{1}{3} = 5\frac{1}{2} - \frac{1}{3} = 5\frac{3}{6} - \frac{2}{6} = 5\frac{1}{6}$

TEST 10

Using your notebooks for working out, ADD:

a) $\frac{1}{9} + \frac{7}{9}$ = ☐

b) $\frac{2}{5} + \frac{2}{3}$ = ☐

c) $\frac{5}{8} + \frac{1}{2}$ = ☐

d) $\frac{5}{6} + \frac{1}{9}$ = ☐

e) $1\frac{1}{2} + \frac{2}{3}$ = ☐

f) $2\frac{3}{7} + 3\frac{1}{2}$ = ☐

g) $7\frac{1}{8} + 3\frac{5}{6}$ = ☐

h) $6\frac{1}{4} + 2\frac{5}{9}$ = ☐

Using your notebooks for working out, SUBTRACT:

i) $\frac{7}{8} - \frac{1}{2}$ = ☐

j) $\frac{3}{4} - \frac{1}{3}$ = ☐

k) $\frac{5}{8} - \frac{1}{2}$ = ☐

l) $\frac{8}{11} - \frac{2}{3}$ = ☐

m) $\frac{11}{15} - \frac{3}{5}$ = ☐

n) $2\frac{3}{4} - 1\frac{3}{10}$ = ☐

o) $3\frac{1}{3} - 1\frac{1}{2}$ = ☐

p) $5\frac{3}{8} - 2\frac{5}{6}$ = ☐

q) $7\frac{5}{11} - 4\frac{2}{3}$ = ☐

TEACHER'S TIP
Don't forget to include the whole number all the way through the sum.

MULTIPLYING FRACTIONS

This is simply done by multiplying the numerators together and multiplying the denominators together.

RULE: Before multiplying anything, first look at the numerator and denominator to see if there is a common factor and then cancel them. Where the numbers are large, then cancelling them down will make the sum easier.

SUM 1 $\frac{3}{5} \times \frac{15}{21}$

METHOD $\frac{3^1 \times \cancel{15}^3}{5_1 \times \cancel{21}_7} = \frac{3}{7}$

Step 1 Find the HCF = 3 and 5. 5 goes into 15 three times and 3 goes into 21 seven times. Then cancel.

• If a MIXED NUMBER is involved, you will need to change it to an improper fraction, before cancelling can begin.

SUM 2 $2\frac{1}{2} \times \frac{3}{5}$

METHOD $2^1/_2 = \frac{5}{2}$

$\frac{5^1 \times 3}{2 \times 5_1} = \frac{3}{2}$

Step 1 First turn the mixed number into an improper fraction (see page 22).
Step 2 Find the common factor (5), then cancel.
Step 3 Now turn it back into a mixed number (see page 22).

ANSWER $1^1/_2$

DIVIDING FRACTIONS

If we divide 3 by 2, the answer is $1^1/_2$.
'2' may be written as $^2/_1$. To divide 3 by $^2/_1$ we could write the sum as $3 \div ^2/_1$. In order to divide this figure, first you must change the $\div$ to a x and invert the second fraction (turn it upside down).
So $3 \div ^2/_1$ becomes: $3 \times ^1/_2 = ^3/_2 = 1^1/_2$.

SUM 1 $^6/_9 \div ^2/_3$

METHOD $\frac{6^3}{9_3} \times \frac{3^1}{2_1} = \frac{3}{3} = 1$

Step 1 First change the sign and invert the second fraction. so $\div ^2/_3$ becomes $\times ^3/_2$. Then find the HCF = 3 and 2.

Step 2 Now cancel = $^3/_3$ or 1 (remember cancel top and bottom).

SUM 2 $3^1/_2 \div 5^1/_4$

METHOD $\frac{7}{2} \div \frac{21}{4}$

$\frac{7^1}{2_1} \times \frac{4^2}{21_3} = \frac{2}{3}$

Step 1 First change the mixed numbers to improper fractions (see page 22).
Step 2 Change the sign and invert the second fraction.
Step 3 Find the HCF (2 and 7) and cancel.

MULTIPLY:

a) $\frac{2}{7} \times \frac{3}{4}$ =

b) $\frac{7}{8} \times \frac{10}{21}$ =

c) $\frac{5}{9} \times \frac{12}{25}$ =

d) $\frac{6}{8} \times \frac{4}{9}$ =

e) $\frac{3}{11} \times \frac{44}{51}$ =

f) $\frac{3}{11} \times \frac{44}{48}$ =

g) $1\frac{1}{11} \times 2\frac{4}{9}$ =

h) $1\frac{3}{15} \times 1\frac{1}{2}$ =

i) $2\frac{1}{2} \times 1\frac{3}{20}$ =

j) $3\frac{1}{5} \times 3\frac{3}{4}$ =

k) $\frac{2}{3} \times 1\frac{7}{8}$ =

l) $8\frac{1}{3} \times 3\frac{3}{5}$ =

DIVIDE:

m) $\frac{2}{3} \div 1\frac{7}{8}$ =

n) $\frac{2}{3} \div 8$ =

o) $\frac{3}{7} \div \frac{9}{14}$ =

p) $\frac{12}{13} \div \frac{4}{26}$ =

q) $\frac{8}{9} \div \frac{12}{21}$ =

r) $\frac{50}{63} \div \frac{15}{7}$ =

s) $\frac{2}{7} \div 1\frac{1}{7}$ =

t) $1\frac{6}{7} \div 1\frac{6}{20}$ =

u) $6\frac{1}{2} \div 1\frac{11}{15}$ =

v) $7\frac{1}{6} \div 1\frac{2}{18}$ =

w) $8\frac{3}{4} \div \frac{15}{28}$ =

x) $12\frac{1}{2} \div 10\frac{5}{6}$ =

TEACHER'S TIP
- REMEMBER: When dividing fractions, change the sign and invert the second fraction.
- Don't forget cancelling means dividing top and bottom lines by the same common factor. DO NOT cancel two top lines or two bottom lines by the HCF.

Like a fraction (see pages 22–27) a **DECIMAL** is also part of something. It may also be called a decimal fraction, where the denominator is a multiple of 10, i.e. 10, 100 or 1000. Just as we have Th, H, T and U for whole numbers, so for decimals we have tenths, hundredths and thousandths. The decimal form for a tenth is 0.1, for a hundredth 0.01 and a thousandth 0.001.

When set out according to place value a decimal will look something like this:

Th	H	T	U	Point	Tenths	Hundredths	Thousandths
1	2	3	4	.	5	0	7

This number is read as one thousand, two hundred and thirty-four point five zero seven (NEVER say point five hundred and seven).

As a decimal number it is written **1234.507**.

ADDING DECIMALS

When writing down an addition sum, it is essential that the decimal points are written vertically, thus keeping the correct value of each place.

SUM 1   **24.2 + 3.74**

METHOD

```
    T  U . Te Hu
    2  4 . 2
 +     3 . 7 4
    2  7 . 9 4
```

Step 1 Write out the sum according to place value.
Step 2 Once the sum is written correctly simply add up the numbers, keeping the decimal point in the same place.

SUBTRACTING DECIMALS

Just as for addition, the points are placed one below the other and we subtract.

SUM 1   **0.257 − 0.164**

METHOD

```
    U . Te Hu Th
    0 . 12 15 7
 −  0 . 1  6  4
    0 . 0  9  3
```

Step 1 Write out the sum according to place value.
Step 2 Once the sum is written correctly simply subtract the numbers, keeping the decimal point in the same place.

SUM 2   **2.46 − 0.013**

Where there is a zero after the decimal point, be sure to put it in its place in the tenths column. NEVER leave a zero out.

METHOD

```
    U . Te Hu Th
    2 . 4  65 10
 −  0 . 0  1  3
    2 . 4  4  7
```

Write in FIGURES:

a) Two hundred and sixty-seven point one five eight

b) Sixteen thousand, one hundred and twenty-five point zero two four

c) Seven thousand, eight hundred point one seven five

d) Eighteen point zero six nine

e) Twelve point two seven

Write in WORDS:

f) 24.25   = ...

g) 327.247   = ...

h) 2120.017 = ...

ADD the following – don't forget to put the decimal point in the answer:

i) 16.253
+28.176
_____

j) 274.001
+362.125
_____

k) 7432.1643
+ 242.3261
_____

Write out the following sums (as shown above) and add them up:

l) 324.67 + 228.75   =

m) 17.241 + 268.13   =

n) 2754.28 + 12.376 =

SUBTRACT the following:

o) 0.89
− 0.52
____

p) 605.17
− 403.06
_____

q) 426.173
− 124.423
_____

Write out the following (as shown above) and subtract:

r) 36.471 − 25.622   =

s) 279.13 − 109.245   =

t) 637.179 − 548.277 =

MULTIPLYING DECIMALS

When we multiplied numbers without a decimal point by 10 or 100, we moved the numbers one or two places to the left. We do the same when multiplying decimals.

For example, 104.6 x 10: by moving the 6 one place to the left, it becomes 1046. Similarly, 27.041 x 100: by moving the 041 two places to the left, it becomes 2704.1.

• Multiplying decimals by another decimal:

SUM 1   **6.4 x 2.4**

METHOD

$$
\begin{array}{r}
\textbf{U.Te} \\
\textbf{6.4} \\
\times\ \underline{\textbf{2.4}} \\
2\,5_{\,1}6 \\
1\,2\,8\,0 \\
\underline{1\,5_{\,1}.3\,6}
\end{array}
$$

Step 1 Set out the sum according to place value. Ignore the decimal point and imagine that you are multiplying 64 by 24 = 1536.

Step 2 Because you were in fact multiplying decimals, you must put the point back in. Now count the number of digits after the decimal point in the numbers of the sum: 6.4 has one digit after the point and 2.4 also has one digit after the point. That makes a total of two digits after the point.

Step 3 Put the point in the answer so that it has two digits after the point, thus 15.36.

• Multiplying decimals by a non-decimal:

SUM 2   **2.7 x 8**

METHOD

$$
\begin{array}{r}
\textbf{2.7} \\
\times\ \underline{\textbf{8}} \\
\underline{2\,1_{\,5}.6}
\end{array}
$$

Step 1 Set out the sum according to place value and multiply.

Step 2 Put the decimal point back in. In this case there is only one digit after the decimal point. So 2.7 x 8 = 21.6.

DIVIDING DECIMALS

When dividing decimals we move the numbers to the right.
For example, 104.6 ÷ 10: by moving the 4 one place to the right, it becomes 10.46. Similarly, 200.025 ÷ 100: by moving the 00 two places to the right, it becomes 2.00025.

• Dividing by decimals:

In order to divide by fractions you must first make them into whole numbers by multiplying by a multiple of 10. To maintain the balance multiply the dividend (the number being divided) by the same.

SUM 1   **50.568 ÷ 0.07**

METHOD

0.07 x 100 = 7
50.568 x 100 = 5056.8

$$
\begin{array}{r}
7\ |\ \underline{5\,0\,^1 5\,^1 6\,.\,2\,^2 8} \\
7\,2\,2\,.\,4
\end{array}
$$

Step 1 Change the decimal (0.07) into a whole number by multiplying by 100. It becomes 7. Multiply the dividend (50.568) by the same. It becomes 5056.8.

Step 2 Work out the sum: 5056.8 ÷ 7 = 722.4.

MULTIPLY the following by 10, 100:

a) 107.23 x 10   = [   ]   **b)** 63.421 x 100   = [   ]

c) 720.024 x 10   = [   ]   **d)** 28.137 x 100   = [   ]

e) 0.013 x 100   = [   ]   **f)** 0.0002 x 100   = [   ]

Write out the following decimals and MULTIPLY:

g) 16.5 x 2   = [   ]   **h)** 14.3 x 0.4   = [   ]

i) 203.2 x 1.1   = [   ]   **j)** 302 x 1.2   = [   ]

k) 27.4 x 2.4   = [   ]   **l)** 687.2 x 3.5   = [   ]

DIVIDE the following by 10, 100:

m) 206.4 ÷ 10   = [   ]   **n)** 162.85 ÷ 100   = [   ]

o) 29.67 ÷ 10   = [   ]   **p)** 86.3 ÷ 100   = [   ]

q) 2.78 ÷ 100   = [   ]   **r)** 0.27 ÷ 100   = [   ]

DIVIDING BY DECIMALS – convert and divide (use long division if necessary):

s) 549.6 ÷ 1.2   = [   ]

t) 13462 ÷ 0.4   = [   ]

u) 98.752 ÷ 0.08   = [   ]

v) 116.76 ÷ 2.1   = [   ]

w) 86.184 ÷ 1.9   = [   ]

x) 3929.208 ÷ 5.3   = [   ]

DECIMALS TO FRACTIONS

To convert a decimal to a common fraction, write down the figures after the point – this will become the numerator. To find the denominator, write a 1 and add the same amount of zeros as there are figures after the point in the original decimal.

For example,

0.133 becomes $\dfrac{133}{1000}$ (There are three figures after the decimal point in 0.133. So put three zeros after the 1 = $^{133}/_{1000}$)

1.23 becomes $\dfrac{23}{100}$ (There are two figures after the decimal point in 1.23. So put two zeros after the 1 = $^{23}/_{100}$)

0.24 becomes $\dfrac{24}{100}$ (This can be reduced to $\dfrac{6}{25}$)

FRACTIONS TO DECIMALS

To convert a common fraction to a decimal fraction, simply divide the numerator by the denominator, adding zeros until the sum is complete.

For example,

$$\frac{1}{2} = 2\overline{\left|\begin{array}{l} 1.\ ^10 \\ 0.\ \ 5 \end{array}\right.} \qquad \frac{1}{4} = 4\overline{\left|\begin{array}{l} 1.\ ^10\ ^20 \\ 0.\ 2\ \ 5 \end{array}\right.} \qquad \frac{1}{3} = 3\overline{\left|\begin{array}{l} 1.\ ^10\ ^10\ ^10 \\ 0.\ 3\ \ 3\ \ 3 \end{array}\right.}$$

In the last sum, you could continue adding 3s indefinitely. This is called a recurring decimal and you signify the recurrence of the 3 by placing a dot above the 3.

So, $^1/_3 = 0.\dot{3}$

$^1/_7 = 1 \div 7 = 0.142857142857142857$
This is also a recurring decimal and a dot is used twice to indicate where the repeated figures begin and end.

So, $^1/_7 = 0.\dot{1}4285\dot{7}$

ORDERING DECIMALS

This is very straightforward – the highest number in the place furthest to the left is the largest.

For example, these fractions are in descending order, the largest first:
0.365 > 0.137 > 0.074   (3 is higher than 1 or 0.)
36.421 > 1.25 > 0.087   (36 is higher than 1 or 0.)

Write as COMMON FRACTIONS (in lowest terms):

a) 0.5 = ☐   **b)** 0.35 = ☐   **c)** 0.175 = ☐

d) 0.25 = ☐   **e)** 0.75 = ☐   **f)** 0.4 = ☐

g) 1.33 = ☐   **h)** 6.79 = ☐   **i)** 19.817 = ☐

Change to DECIMAL FRACTIONS, using the sign for recurring if necessary:

j) $^1/_2$ = ☐   **k)** $^3/_4$ = ☐   **l)** $^5/_8$ = ☐

m) $^2/_3$ = ☐   **n)** $^3/_7$ = ☐   **o)** $^4/_9$ = ☐

p) $^3/_5$ = ☐   **q)** $^{17}/_{100}$ = ☐   **r)** $^5/_6$ = ☐

Write in DESCENDING ORDER, largest first:

s) 0.246, 0.401, 0.711 = ☐

t) 0.246, 0.248, 0.348 = ☐

u) 1.2, 0.21, 0.12 = ☐

v) 7.8, 7.81, 7.801 = ☐

w) 3.4, 3.04, 3.004 = ☐

x) 6.5, 6.505, 6.51 = ☐

It is not always necessary or indeed possible to give an exact answer, particularly in measurements. Complicated answers may be given to a certain number of decimal places (i.e. the number of figures after the decimal point). This is known as dp. You may be asked for 1 dp, 2 dp, 3 dp or more.

For example, express **3.2094 to 3 dp**

Step 1 Look at the 3rd figure after the point in 3.20<u>9</u>4 – it is 9.

Step 2 Now look at the 4th figure after the point 3.209<u>4</u> – it is 4.

Step 3 You must now decide whether the 3rd number stays as a 9 or changes. In order to do this you must consider the following: if the 4th figure is 5 or more, then the 3rd number must be rounded up; if, as in this case, the 4th number is less than 5, then the 3rd figure stays the same.

Step 4 So, 3.2094 to 3 dp is 3.209 (4 is less than 5, so 9 stays the same).

To 2 dp it is 3.21 (9 is bigger than 5, so the 0 needs to be rounded up).

To 1 dp it is 3.2 (zero is less than 5, so the 2 stays the same).

TEACHER'S TIP

Unless told to do so, do not give answers with more decimal places than there are numbers in the question.

SIGNIFICANT FIGURE APPROXIMATION

The method is similar to decimal places, but take care not to mix them up. **SIGNIFICANT FIGURES** (sf) apply to the total number of figures in the question NOT just those after the decimal point. The things to look out for are:

1) The first significant figure of any number is the first figure that is not zero e.g. in 3.2094, the first sf is 3.

2) The second, third and fourth significant figures are simply those that follow the first: this applies to ALL figures, including zeros.

In the number 3.2094, 2094 are the second, third, fourth and fifth significant figures.

For example,

If the original number is 3.2094
Rounded to 4 sf it is 3.209
Rounded to 3 sf it is 3.21
Rounded to 2 sf it is 3.2
Rounded to 1 sf it is 3

If the original number is 365.27
Rounded to 4 sf it is 365.3
Rounded to 3 sf it is 365
Rounded to 2 sf it is 370
Rounded to 1 sf it is 400

If the original number is 0.008357
Rounded to 4 sf it is 0.008357
Rounded to 3 sf it is 0.00836
Rounded to 2 sf it is 0.0084
Rounded to 1 sf it is 0.008

Give the following numbers correct to (i) 3, (ii) 2 and (iii) 1 DECIMAL PLACES:

a) 2.8739
(i) ....
(ii) ....
(iii) ....

b) 67.2563
(i) ....
(ii) ....
(iii) ....

c) 20.09135
(i) ....
(ii) ....
(iii) ....

d) 254.1538
(i) ....
(ii) ....
(iii) ....

e) 0.008729
(i) ....
(ii) ....
(iii) ....

f) 0.0009215
(i) ....
(ii) ....
(iii) ....

Give the following numbers correct to (i) 3, (ii) 2 and (iii) 1 SIGNIFICANT FIGURES:

g) 3.2786
(i) ....
(ii) ....
(iii) ....

h) 7.3092
(i) ....
(ii) ....
(iii) ....

i) 68.015
(i) ....
(ii) ....
(iii) ....

j) 253.926
(i) ....
(ii) ....
(III) ....

k) 1250
(i) ....
(ii) ....
(iii) ....

l) 2095
(i) ....
(ii) ....
(iii) ....

Estimate each number to 1 SIGNIFICANT FIGURE and multiply, to give an approximate answer. (E.g. 376 x 29 is approximately 400 x 30 = 12000)

m) 678 x 19 = [   ]

n) 901 x 38 = [   ]

o) $\dfrac{3.37 \times 4.98}{5.27}$ = [   ]

p) $(1.8)^3$ = [   ]

'**PER CENT**' means per hundred. This means a percentage is a fraction whose denominator is 100. A percentage is written as %.

For example, sixty seven per cent is written as 67%. It means the same as $\frac{67}{100}$ as a common fraction or 0.67 as a decimal.

These are called equivalences.

> **RULE:** To change a fraction to a percentage, multiply by 100% $\left(\frac{100}{1}\right)$

SUM 1   **Express $\frac{7}{20}$ as a percentage in its lowest terms**

METHOD $\frac{7}{20} \times \frac{100}{1}$ %

> **Step 1** Write out the sum according to the rule above – multiply $^7/_{20}$ by $^{100}/_1$.

$\frac{7}{20_1} \times \frac{100^5}{1}$ % $= \frac{35}{1}$

> **Step 2** Cancel.

ANSWER   **35%**
35% can also be expressed as 0.35 as a decimal.

EXPRESS A PERCENTAGE AS A FRACTION

SUM 1   **Express 48% as a fraction in its lowest terms**

METHOD $48\% = \frac{48}{100}$

> **Step 1** Write out sum. 48% as a fraction = $^{48}/_{100}$ (48 per 100).

$\frac{48^{12}}{100_{25}} = \frac{12}{25}$

> **Step 2** Cancel.

ANSWER $\frac{12}{25}$
48% can also be expressed as 0.48 as a decimal.

EXPRESS A DECIMAL AS A FRACTION

For example,

$0.25 = \frac{25}{100} = 25\%$ $\qquad\qquad 0.5 = \frac{50}{100} = 50\%$

$1.73 = \frac{173}{100} = 173\%$

TEST 16

Express the following as COMMON FRACTIONS in their lowest terms:

a) 45% = ☐   **b)** 5% = ☐   **c)** 15% = ☐

d) 40% = ☐   **e)** 44% = ☐   **f)** 64% = ☐

Express the following as PERCENTAGES:

g) 0.75 = ☐   **h)** 0.27 = ☐   **i)** 0.09 = ☐

j) 1.25 = ☐   **k)** 0.125 = ☐   **l)** 0.075 = ☐

Express as i) a COMMON FRACTION and ii) as a DECIMAL FRACTION:

m) 12%   **n)** 30%   **o)** 8%
(i) ....   (i) ....   (i) ....
(ii) ....   (ii) ....   (ii) ....

Express the following as PERCENTAGES:

p) $\frac{1}{2}$ = ☐   **q)** $\frac{3}{10}$ = ☐   **r)** $\frac{13}{20}$ = ☐

s) $\frac{7}{5}$ = ☐   **t)** $\frac{21}{25}$ = ☐   **u)** $\frac{7}{8}$ = ☐

Fill in the gaps: **v)**

FRACTION	PERCENTAGE	DECIMAL
3/4		
	60%	
		0.55
4/5		
		0.3

If we want to find 20 as a percentage of 25, we know that 20 is a twentieth part of 25 ($^{20}/_{25}$). To make it into a percentage multiply by $\underline{100}$ (see page 36).
$\quad$ 1

So, $\dfrac{20}{25_1} \times \dfrac{\cancel{100}^4}{1} \%\ = 80\%$

To express one quantity as a percentage of another, divide the first quantity by the second and multiply this fraction by 100%.

SUM 1   **Express 7cm as a percentage of 20cm**

METHOD $\dfrac{7}{20} \times \dfrac{100}{1}$

Step 1 Write the sum expressing a seventh of 20 as $^7/_{20}$. Now multiply by $^{100}/_1$ (see page 36).

$\dfrac{7}{20_1} \times \dfrac{\cancel{100}^5}{1} = \dfrac{35}{1} = 35\%$

Step 2 Cancel and write the answer as a percentage.

• When dealing with measures, first ensure all measurements are in the same units before making a fraction.

SUM 2   **Calculate 84g as a percentage of 1kg**

METHOD $\dfrac{84}{1000} \times \dfrac{100}{1}$

Step 1 Make all measurements the same – change the 1kg to 1000g and write as a fraction of 1000 = $^{84}/_{1000}$. Now multiply by $^{100}/_1$.

$\dfrac{84}{1000_{10}} \times \dfrac{\cancel{100}^1}{1} = \dfrac{84}{10} = 8.4\%$

Step 2 Cancel and write the answer as a percentage.

• To find a percentage of a quantity write the percentage as a fraction, change the 'of' to a multiplication sign and put the quantity over 1.

SUM 3   **Find 15% of 360.**

METHOD $\dfrac{15}{100} \times \dfrac{360}{1}$

Step 1 Write 15% as $^{15}/_{100}$ and substitute an 'x' for 'of'.
Step 2 Write down the quantity (360) and put it over 1.
Step 3 Cancel down to get the answer = 54.

$\dfrac{\cancel{15}^3}{\cancel{100}_{20_1}} \times \dfrac{\cancel{360}^{18}}{1} = \dfrac{54}{1} = 54$

SUM 4   **If 76% of the 25 pupils in a class can swim, how many can't swim?**

METHOD $100 - 76\% = 24\%$

$\dfrac{24}{100} \times \dfrac{25}{1}$

$\dfrac{24}{100_4} \times \dfrac{\cancel{25}^1}{1} = \dfrac{24}{4} = 6$

Step 1 First you must find what percentage of children cannot swim: 100 − 76 = 24.
Step 2 You now know that 24% out of 25 cannot swim. Put this into fraction form $^{24}/_{100}$ x by quantity (25) over 1 = $^{25}/_1$.
Step 3 Cancel $^{24}/_4$ = 6 children cannot swim.

Express the first quantity as a PERCENTAGE of the second:

a) 3, 15 = ☐

b) 4, 20 = ☐

c) 24, 40 = ☐

d) 13mm, 3cm = ☐

e) 284g, 1kg = ☐

f) 800m, 2km = ☐

g) 45p, £1.50 = ☐

h) 75cm, 3m = ☐

i) 5in, 12in = ☐

Find the VALUE of the following:

j) 40% of 90 = ☐

k) 16% of 800 = ☐

l) 7% of £13 = ☐

m) 63% of 75l = ☐

n) 85% of 48m = ☐

o) 96% of 225g = ☐

p) If 72% of cars were new, what percentage were not new? ☐

q) There are 80 photographs in an album.
If 85% are in colour, how many are in black and white? ☐

r) In a school of 420, 65% come to school by bus.
How many do not come by bus? ☐

TEACHER'S TIP
A whole or 1 is represented by 100%.

18. PERCENTAGES 3

The original value of anything is 100%. If you want to increase a figure by a percentage amount, you will need to increase the 100%.

SUM 1 **Increase 400 by 36%**

METHOD **136% of 400**

$$\frac{136}{100} \times \frac{400}{1}$$

$$\frac{136}{100_1} \times \frac{400^4}{1} = \frac{544}{1} = 544$$

Step 1 400 is already 100% so in order to increase it by 36%, you must add it to the 100%. Therefore the new value will become 136% of 400.

Step 2 Write the sum as a fraction and multiply by $^{400}/_1$.

Step 3 Cancel.

• Similarly, when you need to decrease a figure by a percentage amount, you will need to reduce the 100%.

SUM 2 **Decrease 400 by 36%**

METHOD **100% − 36% = 64% of 400**

$$\frac{64}{100} \times \frac{400}{1}$$

$$\frac{64}{100_1} \times \frac{400^4}{1} = \frac{256}{1} = 256$$

Step 1 In order to decrease 400 by 36%, you must decrease the 100% by 36%. The new value will be 64% of 400.

Step 2 Write the sum as a fraction and multiply by $^{400}/_1$.

Step 3 Cancel.

• To find the percentage change when you know the original value, you must make your fraction by putting 'the change' over the original.

SUM 3 **If a shopkeeper bought a coat for £40 and sold it for £65, what was his percentage profit?**

METHOD **£65 − £40 = £25 profit**

$$\frac{25}{40} \times \frac{100}{1}$$

$$\frac{25}{40_2} \times \frac{100^5}{1} = \frac{125}{2} = 62\frac{1}{2}\%$$

Step 1 First find the amount of profit ('the change'): 65 − 40 = 25.

Step 2 Now write as a fraction, putting the change (or profit) over the original = $^{25}/_{40}$ and multiply by $^{100}/_1$.

Step 3 Cancel.

• There are situations where a percentage increase or decrease occurs.

If you deposit £700 in a Building Society account for 1 year with an interest of 4% pa, how much would you have at the end of the year?

$$\frac{104}{100_1} \times \frac{700^7}{1} = £728$$

If value added tax (VAT) is 17½%, what is the cost of a table priced at £150 plus VAT?

$$\frac{117.5}{100^2} \times \frac{150^3}{1} = \frac{352.5}{2} = £176.25$$

a) Increase 200 by 17% = ☐

b) Decrease 200 by 17% = ☐

c) Alice is 8% heavier than she was three years ago. If she weighed 100lb then, how much does she weigh now? = ☐

d) If I put £300 into a Building Society for one year, at an interest rate of 4% pa, what will it be worth at the end of the year? = ☐

e) If a car that cost £9000 new, decreased in value by 12%, how much would it be worth? = ☐

f) If a shopkeeper buys a lamp for £28 and marks it up by £8.40, what percentage is his profit? = ☐

g) In a sale, a shop offers 30% discount. How much would a carpet marked at £48 cost? = ☐

h) The purchase price of a kettle is £27, before 15% discount. What is the sale price after discount? = ☐

i) Mr Brown receives an increase of £35 on his weekly pay of £175. What percentage is his increase? = ☐

j) An art dealer bought a painting for £700. If he sells it, making a profit of 55%, what is the selling price? = ☐

ALGEBRA is a useful way to solve problems. First of all letters are used to denote particular numbers. These letters may be multiplied by numbers to indicate many of them.

For example, $4x = x + x + x + x$; $3y = y + y + y$

COLLECTING LIKE TERMS

When working out algebra, first put the same letters together – this is called collecting like terms: $2a + 2a = 4a$ ($2a$ and $4a$ are like terms).

SUM 1 $3f + 2g + 5f$

METHOD $3f + 5f + 2g$
$= 8f + 2g$

Step 1 Collect like terms — the 'f's are like terms.
Step 2 Add the like terms together — $5f + 3f = 8f$.

SUM 2   **If $a = 3$, what does $4a$ equal?**

METHOD $4a = 4 \times a$
$= 4 \times 3$
$= 12$

Step 1 Write out the equation in its simplest terms –
$4a = 4$ lots of 'a'.
Step 2 Now replace 'a' with its value (3). Rewrite the equation as 4×3 and work out the sum.

• If you have the value of a letter, you can find the value of the term; however, letters do not always have the same value.

SUM 3   **If $a = 4$ and $b = 5$, find $2a + 3b$**

METHOD $2a + 3b = 2 \times 4 + 3 \times 5$
$= \ \ 8 + 15 = 23$

Step 1 Write out the equation, i.e. $2a + 3b$ and replace each letter with its value – $a = 4$, so $2a = 2 \times 4 = 8$; $b = 5$, so $3b = 3 \times 5 = 15$.
Step 2 Now add them together – $8 + 15 = 23$.

ADDITION AND MULTIPLICATION OF TERMS

Sometimes several terms are multiplied by the same number. This is easily done by the use of brackets. The term outside the brackets multiplies each separate term inside the bracket.

$2(a + b) = 2a + 2b$ $(2 \times a + 2 \times b = 2a + 2b)$
$2a(b + 1) = 2ab + 2a$ $(2a \times b + 2a \times 1 = 2ab + 2a)$
$a(3 - b) = 3a - ab$ $(a \times 3 - a \times b = 3a - ab)$
$-2(x - 1) = -2x + 2$ $(\text{NOTE that } -2 \times -1 = +2)$

• To multiply terms with the same letter, add the indices (see page 20).

$y^2 \times y^2 = y^{2+2} = y^4$ (or $y \times y \times y \times y = y^4$)
$m^2 \times m^6 = m^{2+6} = m^8$
$c^3 \times c^2 = c^{3+2} = c^5$

If we add x^2 and $2x$, remember they are not like terms. To add these two different terms, you simply put a $+$ sign, so $x^2 + 2x$.

COLLECTING LIKE TERMS:

a) $3x + 4x$ = [ ] **b)** $2a + 7a$ = [ ]

c) $2m + 3n$ = [ ] **d)** $4f + 3g + 7f + 2g$ = [ ]

e) $6y + 2x - 2y + 3x$ = [ ] **f)** $12a + 4b - 6a - 2b$ = [ ]

SUBSTITUTE the following numerical values:

g) If $x = 2$, find $4x$ = [ ]

h) If $a = 3$, find $3a - 4$ = [ ]

i) If $a = 2$ and $b = 3$, find $7a + 2b$ = [ ]

j) If $x = 2$, $y = 3$ and $z = 4$, find $7x + 4y - 2z$ = [ ]

k) If $m = 4$ and $n = 5$, find $3m + 4n + 2m - 2n$ = [ ]

l) If $c = 6$ and $d = 7$, find $5c - 2d + 2c$ = [ ]

BRACKETS – simplify the following equations:

m) $3(a + b)$ = [ ] **n)** $2(3 - y)$ = [ ]

o) $4(2b - 5)$ = [ ] **p)** $2x(y + 2)$ = [ ]

q) $-3(9c + 2)$ = [ ] **r)** $-2(p - 4)$ = [ ]

INDICES:

s) $x(y - x)$ = [ ] **t)** $y^2 \times y^2$ = [ ]

u) $a^3 \times a^4 \times a^2$ = [ ]

COLLECTING LIKE TERMS:

v) $a^2 + 5a + 2a^2$ = [ ] **w)** $b^3 + 3b + b^2 + 2b$ = [ ]

x) $c^2 + c + 2c^2 + 2c$ = [ ] **y)** $a^2 + b^2 + 2b^2 + 3b$ = [ ]

z) $m^2 + n^3 + m^2 + 2n^3 + n^2$ = [ ]

TEACHER'S TIP

Like terms: y^2 means $y \times y$ AND $2y$ means $y + y$ BUT $y^2 + 2y$ are NOT like terms.

EQUATIONS

The equals sign in an equation means that the value of the left-hand side (LHS) is exactly the same as that of the right-hand side (RHS). If we treat the LHS and the RHS exactly the same, the two sides will remain equal i.e. we may add to, subtract from, multiply or divide BOTH sides by the same amount and still the LHS = RHS.

SUM 1 **Find a when a + 2 = 6**

METHOD

$$a + 2 = 6$$
$$a + 2 - 2 = 6 - 2$$
$$a = 4$$

Step 1 Write out the equation as given: a + 2 = 6.

Step 2 Now treat each side of the equation in exactly the same way. Take 2 from each side and you can find a.

This method can become cumbersome, so there is a rule:

RULE: Change the side, change the sign: + becomes − and − becomes +.

This refers to the 'job' of a number. In a + 2 = 6 the 2's sign is a plus (+) sign. If we take it to the other side, it takes the sign of minus.

$$a + 2 = 6$$
$$a \quad = 6 - 2$$
$$a \quad = 4$$

Step 1 Write out the equation as given − a + 2 = 6

Step 2 Take +2 to the other side and change its job to −2. You can now find a = 6 − 2 = 4.

Here are some more examples:

1) $4b = 12$
   $$b = \frac{12}{4}$$
   $$b = 3$$

Step 1 Write out the equation as given − 4b = 12.

Step 2 Take x4 to the other side and change its job to ÷4. You can now find b = 12 ÷ 4 = 3.

2) $c + 5 = 9$
   $$c = 9 - 5$$
   $$c = 4$$

3) $d - 3 = 8$
   $$d = 8 + 3$$
   $$d = 11$$

4) $\dfrac{e}{6} = 2$
   $$e = 2 \times 6$$
   $$e = 12$$

Solve the following EQUATIONS:

a) n + 5 = 7

n = ☐

b) p − 3 = 2

p = ☐

c) 4q = 12

q = ☐

d) $\frac{r}{9}$ = 1

r = ☐

e) 4s + 2 = 10

s = ☐

f) 7t − 3 = 11

t = ☐

g) $\frac{12u}{3}$ = 4

u = ☐

h) 9v x 2 = 18

v = ☐

i) 2w − 3 = 18 − 5w

w = ☐

j) 3x − 2 + 2x = 13

x = ☐

TEACHER'S TIP
Anything TIMES 0 = 0,
i.e. 1 x 0 = 0, 200 x 0 = 0, M x 0 = 0.

Some equations have letters on both sides. Before solving the equation it is necessary to collect all the letters on one side and the numbers on the other side (collecting like terms).

SUM 1 **Find g when 5g + 3 = 2g + 9**

METHOD

$$5g - 2g = 9 - 3$$
$$3g = 6$$
$$g = \frac{6}{3}$$

ANSWER **g = 2**

Step 1 Collect like terms – the 5g and 9 stay as they are. Move the +3 and 2g to the other side and change their signs – they both become minus. So 5g – 2g = 9 – 3. Now work out the sum: 3g = 6.

Step 2 To find g, take the x3 to the other side and change its job (sign) to ÷. Now you can find g = 6 ÷ 3 = 2.

SUM 2 **Find k when $\frac{3k}{4}$ = −9**

METHOD

$$3k = -9 \times 4$$
$$3k = -36$$
$$k = \frac{-36}{3}$$

ANSWER **k = −12**

Step 1 To find k: move the ÷4 to the other side and change its job (sign) to multiply. Work out this sum: 3k = −9 x 4 = −36. To find k, move the x3 to the other side and change its sign to ÷.

Step 2 Now you can find k = −36 ÷ 3 = −12.

• Some equations have brackets:

SUM 3 **Find h when 5(3h − 2) = 20**

METHOD

$$15h - 10 = 20$$
$$15h = 20 + 10$$
$$15h = 30$$
$$h = \frac{30}{15}$$

Step 1 First work out the value of the figures in brackets – 5 x 3h = 15h, 5 x 2 = 10. Write out the equation as shown: 15h – 10 = 20.

Step 2 Move the −10 to the other side and change its job (sign) from − to +, and work out the sum 15h = 20 + 10 = 30. So 15h = 30.

Step 3 To find h, take the x15 to the other side and change its job (sign) to ÷. Work out the sum: h = 30 ÷ 15 = 2.

ANSWER **h = 2**

• Some equations have indices:

SUM 4 **Find m when 5m² + 3 = 48**

METHOD

$$5m^2 = 48 - 3$$
$$5m^2 = 45$$
$$m^2 = \frac{45}{5}$$
$$m^2 = 9$$
$$m = \pm 3$$

Step 1 First take the +3 to the other side and change its job (sign) to −. Work out the sum − 5m² = 48 − 3 = 45.

Step 2 Now find m², by taking the 5 to the other side and changing its job (sign) to divide. Work out the sum: m² = 45 ÷ 5 = 9. To find m, you need to find the root of 9 = ±3.

ANSWER **± 3**

(± means plus or minus i.e. m² could mean 3 x 3 or −3 x −3)

a) $2y = 12 - 2y$ $y = \boxed{}$

b) $8 - 4 = 6z - 8z$ $z = \boxed{}$

c) $3(3a + 1) = 30$ $a = \boxed{}$

d) $2(3b - 4) = 5(b - 1)$ $b = \boxed{}$

e) $7(b - 4) = 5(b - 2)$ $b = \boxed{}$

f) $5(c - 2) = 3(c + 6)$ $c = \boxed{}$

g) $3(4d - 2) = 3(d - 2)$ $d = \boxed{}$

h) $4e - 3(2e - 2) = 3(e + 8)$ $e = \boxed{}$

i) $5(1 + f) + 8 = 3(f - 1)$ $f = \boxed{}$

j) $2x(3 - 4) = 4(5 - x)$ $x = \boxed{}$

k) $2(3g + 1) = 2g(2 + 4)$ $g = \boxed{}$

SUBSTITUTING IN FORMULAE

A formula is a 'recipe' using algebra to make it easy to work something out by simply substituting a number for a letter.

To convert °C into °F, the formula is: $F = \dfrac{9C}{5} + 32$

SUM 1   Find 20°C in F°

METHOD

$F = \dfrac{9C}{5} + 32$

Step 1 Write out the formula as above.

$F = \dfrac{9 \times 20}{5} + 32$

Step 2 Substitute C for its value of 20 – the rest stays the same.

$F = \dfrac{9 \times \cancel{20}^{4}}{\cancel{5}^{1}} + 32$

Step 3 Cancel.
Step 4 Work out the sum.

$= 36 + 32$

ANSWER   **68°F**

• To convert kilometres to miles, the formula is $m = \dfrac{5k}{8}$

SUM 2   Find how many miles are equal to 32 kilometres

METHOD

$m = \dfrac{5}{8} k$

Step 1 Write out the formula as above.

$m = \dfrac{5 \times 32}{8}$

Step 2 Substitute k for its value of 32.

$m = \dfrac{5 \times \cancel{32}^{4}}{\cancel{8}^{1}}$

Step 3 Cancel.
Step 4 Work out the sum.

$= \dfrac{20}{1}$

ANSWER   **20 miles**

CONSTRUCTING FORMULAE

When you are given a problem in the form of a written sentence, you will need to construct a formula.

SUM 1   Hannah is one-third of her mother's age and both their ages together add up to 52. Find the ages of Hannah and her mother.

METHOD

$x + 3x = 52$
$4x = 52$
$x = \dfrac{52}{4}$

Step 1 First work out a formula. Let x be Hannah's age. If her mother is 3 times older, then let her mother's age be 3x. You know that Hannah's age + her mother's age = 52. So 4x = 52. To find x, take the 4 to the other side and change its job (sign) to ÷. Now work out the sum. 52 ÷ 4 = 13. If Hannah is 13, her mother must be 3 times this, i.e. 39. (39 + 13 = 52)

ANSWER   **Hannah is 13, her mother is 39**

SUBSTITUTING IN A FORMULA:

a) Find v, if u = 6 and t = 3

$v = \dfrac{u - t}{3}$

v = ☐

b) Find c when r = 3 and t = −4

c = rt

c = ☐

c) Find a when b = 1, c = 2 and d = 3

a = b + cd

a = ☐

d) Find w when z = 25

$w = \dfrac{z}{100}$

w = ☐

e) If r = 2 and t = 3, find p

p = r(2t − 5)

p = ☐

f) Find r, if s = 2 and t = 3

$r = \dfrac{2}{s + t}$

r = ☐

CONSTRUCTING FORMULAE:

g) If I buy 2 books at £s each and 3 books at £t each, how many pounds change will I have from £20?

h) The cost to stay at a hotel for an adult is £2x per day. A child is charged at half the adult rate. Find the cost, c, of the total bill for a week for a family of two adults and three children.

i) During one week a secretary posted 'e' letters with 27p stamps and 'f' letters with 19p stamps. What was the postage cost 'c' for that week?

TEACHER'S TIP

Always start by writing the formula. Even though you change only one letter to a number, write all the expressions at each stage.

CHANGING THE SUBJECT OF A FORMULA

This is similar to solving equations.

SUM 1   If $x + y = z$, find x

METHOD $x = z - y$

Step 1 To get the value of x, move y to the other side and change its job (sign) (+y becomes –y).

SUM 2   If $r = st$, find s

METHOD $\dfrac{r}{t} = s$

Step 1 To get the value of s, move t to the other side and change its job (sign) (xt becomes ÷t).

SUM 3   If $e = fg - fd$, find f

METHOD $e = f(g - d)$

$\dfrac{e}{(g - d)} = f$

Step 1 Find the common factor: f (it is common to both terms). Collect like terms and write the formula as shown.
Step 2 To find the value of f, move the g and d to the other side and change their job (signs) from x to ÷.

TOP OF THE TREE

The following algebraic formula is of a higher level than those previously illustrated, but it is worth having a look. You never know, you may find it easy!

SUM 1   If $x = y + \frac{1}{2} z$, find z

METHOD $x - y = \frac{1}{2} z$

$x - y \div \frac{1}{2} = z$
$2(x - y) = z$

Step 1 Move y to the other side and change its job (sign) (+y becomes –y). To find z you must also move the $\frac{1}{2}$ to the other side and change its sign.
Step 2 In fractions you cannot divide by $\frac{1}{2}$. So you must change the ÷ sign to a x sign and invert the fraction (see pages 26–27).

CHANGING THE SUBJECT OF A FORMULA:

a) Make 'b' the subject of

$\frac{a}{x} + b = 1$

= ....

b) Make 'b' the subject of

$6abc = 9a^2c$

= ....

c) Make 'w' the subject of

$y = 3w - z$

= ....

d) Make 'f' the subject of

$g = \frac{2f}{3}$

= ....

e) Make 'a' the subject of

$ax + 2ay + 3az = 9$

= ....

f) Make 'y' the subject of

$\frac{y^2}{9} = c^2$

= ....

g) Make 'b' the subject of

$a = 2b + c$

= ....

h) Make 'p' the subject of

$q = r + \frac{p}{5}$

= ....

i) Make 'v' the subject of

$v = 2v + 3u$

= ....

When looking at positive and negative numbers we discovered that a number is bigger than another number if it is on the right-hand side of the number value line (see pages 18–19).

Inequalities are like equalities except that the unknown has a range of values. For example, x > 5 means that x can be something greater than 5 but, x = 5 means that x is exactly 5.

On a number line x > 5

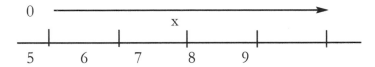

We use an open circle 0 to denote that x cannot be equal to 5.

On a number line x ≥ 5

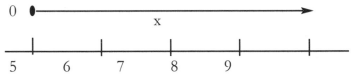

We use a solid circle to denote that x MAY equal 5.

• An inequality remains true when the same number is ADDED TO or SUBTRACTED FROM both sides.

SUM 1   **Find x where   x + 6 < 2**

METHOD   **x < 2 − 6**

x < −4

Step 1 As in equations (see pages 42–47), in order to find x you must move the 6 to the other side and change its sign.
Step 2 Work out the sum: 2 − 6 = −4. Remember that with inequalities the signs (e.g. greater than/less than) remain the same throughout.

• An inequality also remains true when both sides are multiplied or divided by a POSITIVE number.

SUM 2   **Find x where   2x − 2 > 4**

METHOD   **2x − 2 > 4**

2x > 4 + 2

2x > 6

$$x > \frac{6}{2} = x > 3$$

Step 1 As before, write out the inequality. To find x, you must move the 2 to the other side and change its sign to +2. To find x, you must move the x2 to the other side, where it becomes ÷2.
Step 2 Work out the sum — the signs stay the same.

• An inequality, multiplied or divided by a NEGATIVE number reverses the inequality sign.

SUM 3   **Multiply 6 < 10 by −2**

METHOD   **−12 < −20**

−12 > −20

−3 < −5

−3 > −5

Step 1 Multiply both sides by −2. The inequality now reads −12 < −20. This is NOT true, so reverse the inequality sign.
This inequality is now TRUE.
This inequality is NOT true.
This inequality IS true.

TEST 24

Use a NUMBER LINE with open or solid circles to represent the values of x:

a) $x > 3 =$

b) $x \leq 5 =$

c) $x > -2 =$

d) $x < 0 =$

Rewrite these using INEQUALITY LINES:

e) x is more than 6 but less than 12

f) y is more than 10 but less than 12

g) z is not more than 14 and not less than 5

Solve the following and illustrate the solutions on NUMBER LINES:

h) $x - 3 < 9 =$

i) $x + 4 > 5 =$

j) $x - 5 < -3 =$

k) $x + 6 < 0 =$

TEACHER'S TIP
The < and > signs remain the same throughout. But the + and – signs still change.

A ratio shows the connection between two quantities. This is always in PROPORTION. Ratios can be simplified by dividing by the **HCF**.

When simplifying ratios, both amounts need to be in the same units.

SUM 1 **Simplify 60p : £1.08**

METHOD **60 : 108**

$^5\cancel{60} : \cancel{108}^9 = 60 : 108 :: 5 : 9$

Step 1 First change £1.08 to pence = 108.
Step 2 Rewrite the ratio, find the HCF = 12 and simplify.

SUM 2 **Simplify 300g : 1.5kg**

METHOD **300 : 1500**

$^1\cancel{300} : \cancel{1500}^5 = 300 : 1500 :: 1 : 5$

Step 1 First change the kilograms to grams.
Step 2 Find the HCF = 300 and simplify.

TO MAKE A RATIO EQUATION

RULE: The product of the inner numbers is equal to the product of the outer numbers.

20 : 6 :: 10 : 3	6 x 10 = 20 x 3 = 60
60 : 108 :: 5 : 9	108 x 5 = 60 x 9 = 540
300 : 1500 :: 1 : 5	1500 x 1 = 300 x 5 = 1500

SUM 1 **Find how much petrol a car uses to travel 60km, when it uses 4 litres to travel 75km.**

METHOD **4 : 75 :: x : 60**

Step 1 Lay the equation out in order.
So litres (4) : distance (75) :: litres (x) : distance (60), where x is the unknown quantity.

$75x = 4 \times 60$

$x = \dfrac{4 \times 60^{\cancel{12}\,4}}{75^{\cancel{15}\,5}}$

Step 2 Lay out the equation according to the rule – product of inners (75 x x) = product of outers (4 x 60).
Step 3 Now simplify to find x.

$x = \dfrac{4 \times 4}{5} \quad x = \dfrac{16}{5}$

ANSWER **3.2 litres**

SUM 2 **An advertisement in a newspaper costs 80 pence for 5 words. How much will it cost for 18 words?**

METHOD **80 : 5 :: x : 18**

Step 1 Lay the ratio out in order – money : words :: money : words, using x for the unknown quantity.

$5x = 18 \times 80$

Step 2 Lay out the equation according to rule – product of inners = product of outers.
Step 3 Now simplify to find x.

$x = \dfrac{18 \times 80^{16}}{\cancel{5}_1}$

$x = 18 \times 16 = 288 \text{ pence}$

ANSWER **£2.88**

SIMPLIFY in lowest terms:

a) 12 : 4 :: ☐

b) 7 : 35 :: ☐

c) 12 : 15 :: ☐

d) 27 : 6 :: ☐

e) 20p : £1.04 :: ☐

f) 20cm : 1m :: ☐

g) 55ml : 1l :: ☐

h) 10in : 8ft :: ☐

i) 48g : 1kg :: ☐

j) 260m : 1.5km :: ☐

Lay out each of the following as a RATIO EQUATION and solve:

k) A farmer walks for four hours covering 18km. How long did he take to cover 12 km? (Give the answer in hours and minutes.)

....

l) A carpet costs £156 for 12m^2. What is the cost of 7m^2?

....

m) 4 people can stay in a hotel for 5 days for £560. How much will it cost them to stay for a week?

....

n) If I invest £500, I receive £15 interest. How much would the interest be if I invest £900?

....

o) The scale model of a ship is such that the mast is 12cm high and the mast of the original ship is 9m high. The length of the original ship is 33m. How long is the model ship?

....

TEACHER'S TIP

- Make all the lengths the same units.
- Always lay the ratio out in order.

Simple number patterns are:

The EVEN **numbers**   **2, 4, 6, 8, 10 etc**

The ODD **numbers**   **1, 3, 5, 7, 9, 11 etc**

The SQUARE **numbers:** **1,   4,   9,   16,   25,   36,   49**
(1x1) (2x2) (3x3) (4x4) (5x5) (6x6) (7x7)

The CUBE **numbers:**   **1,   8,   27,   64,   125**
(1x1x1) (2x2x2) (3x3x3) (4x4x4) (5x5x5)

The TRIANGLE **numbers:** **1,   3,   6,   10,   15,   21**

POWERS OF TEN: **10,   100,   1000,   10000,   100000**
(10^1)   (10^2)   (10^3)   (10^4)   (10^5)

POWERS OF TWO: **2,   4,   8,   16,   32,   64**
(2^1) (2^2) (2^3) (2^4) (2^5) (2^6)

If you are given a few numbers and are asked to CONTINUE THE SEQUENCE, first observe the pattern and follow its rule to find the unknowns.

Find the next two numbers in the following patterns:
Example 1:
5, 10, 15, 20 – – Pattern is plus 5.
Next two are **25 (20 + 5); 30 (25 + 5)**

Example 2:
3, 6, 12, 24 – – Pattern is doubling.
Next two are **48 (24 x 2); 96 (48 x 2)**

Example 3:
1, 4, 7, 10 – – Pattern is adding 3.
Next two are **13 (10 + 3); 16 (13 + 3)**

Look at the pattern and complete it:

a) 10 20 30 40 __ __

b) 21 18 15 12 __ __

c) 17 14 11 8 __ __

d) 2 4 8 16 __ __

e) 1 3 6 10 __ __

f) 1 4 9 16 __ __

g) 50 43 36 29 __ __

h) 5 10 15 __ __

i) 5 7 9 11 __ __

j) 10 14 18 22 __ __

k) 144 72 36 18 __ __

l) 10 100 1000 __ __

m) $\dfrac{1}{2}$ $\dfrac{1}{3}$ $\dfrac{1}{4}$ $\dfrac{1}{5}$ __ __

n) 0.1 0.01 0.001 __ __

o) 0 –2 –4 –6 __ __

p) –10 –7 –4 –1 __ __

q) 8 16 32 64 __ __

r) 24 20 16 12 __ __

s) 132 121 110 99 __ __

t) 36 48 60 72 __ __

u) 5 11 17 23 __ __

v) 0.25 0.5 1 2 __ __

w) 100 50 25 12.5 __ __

x) $\dfrac{1}{2}$ $\dfrac{1}{4}$ $\dfrac{1}{8}$ __ __

THE 'nth' TERM

A sequence can be found from a formula. 'n' is used to stand for the position of a number in a sequence.

For example,
If the formula is **2n + 1**

In the 1st term, the formula reads:
2 x 1 + 1 (substitute 1 for n)
= 3

In the 2nd term, the formula reads:
2 x 2 + 1 (substitute 2 for n)
= 5

In the 3rd term, the formula reads:
2 x 3 + 1 (substitute 3 for n)
= 7

In the 4th term, the formula reads:
2 x 4 + 1 (substitute 4 for n)
= 9
NOTE that the difference between each solution is 2.

• It is important to lay the formula out correctly.

If the formula is **5n − 2**

1st term	2nd term	3rd term	4th term
5 x 1 − 2	5 x 2 − 2	5 x 3 − 2	5 x 4 − 2
= 3	= 8	= 13	= 18

NOTE that the difference between each solution is 5.

SUM 1   **Find the formula when given part of the sequence − 4, 7, 10, 13**

METHOD

1st term	2nd	3rd	4th
4	7	10	13
+3	+3	+3	+3
3(1x3)	6(2x3)	9(3x3)	12(4x3)
1	1	1	1

Step 1 Write out the sequence under 1st, 2nd, 3rd and 4th term headings.
Step 2 Find the difference i.e. 3.
Step 3 Multiply this difference by 'n' and place in the line below the number.
Step 4 Subtract vertically (4 − 3 =1; 7 − 6 = 1; 10 − 9 = 1; 13 − 12 = 1).

ANSWER   The nth term is 3n + 1 as 3n is one short of 4, 7, 10 and 13.
Check that the formula 3n + 1 works for two samples in your sequence.
for n = 3, 3n + 1 = 3 x 3 + 1 = 10 (correct)
for n = 4, 3n + 1 = 3 x 4 + 1 = 13 (correct)

Find the FIRST FOUR terms from each formula:

	1st term	2nd	3rd	4th
a) n + 1	_____	_____	_____	_____
b) 2n	_____	_____	_____	_____
c) 3n	_____	_____	_____	_____
d) n + 4	_____	_____	_____	_____
e) 2n – 1	_____	_____	_____	_____
f) 5n – 5	_____	_____	_____	_____
g) 4n – 3	_____	_____	_____	_____
h) 12 – 2n	_____	_____	_____	_____

Find the FORMULA for each sequence:

i) 1 4 7 10

1st term	2nd	3rd	4th
1	4	7	10

j) 8 13 18 23

k) 5 11 17 23

l) 4 7 10 13

Cartesian geometry is named after the Frenchman Rene Descartes who is said to have had the original idea after watching a fly crawl across a beamed ceiling while he was ill in bed. As he watched the fly he began to think about how he could plot the fly's progress using numbers and lines.

The basis of the system is that points may be denoted by their position in relation to two axes, which cross at zero, or the 'origin' as it is known. The horizontal axis is the 'x' axis; the vertical axis the 'y' axis. Coordinates are given in alphabetical order like this: (x, y).

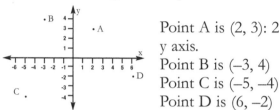

Point A is (2, 3): 2 on the x axis, 3 on the y axis.
Point B is (–3, 4)
Point C is (–5, –4)
Point D is (6, –2)

RULE: Always plot the x coordinate first.

STRAIGHT LINES ON A GRAPH

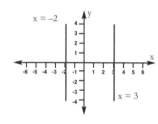

VERTICAL LINES

When **x = 3**, all the points with x coordinate 3 form a straight vertical line, x = 3. Similarly x = –2 is a straight vertical line, but on the minus side of the grid.

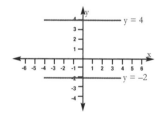

HORIZONTAL LINES

When **y = 4**, all the points with y coordinate 4 form a straight horizontal line, y = 4. Similarly y = –2 is a straight horizontal line but on the minus side of the grid.

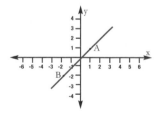

DIAGONAL LINES

When **y = x**, it means all the points with the same x and y coordinates are joined. So (3, 3) (2, 2) (1, 1) (0, 0) (–1, –1) (–2, –2) etc. This forms a diagonal line through the centre of the grid.

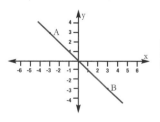

Similarly when **y = –x** (–3, 3) (–2, 2) (–1, 1) (0, 0) (1, –1) (2, –2) are joined, forming a straight diagonal line through the centre of the grid.

a) On the set of axes below, plot and name the following points:
**A(3, 1), B(2, 2), C(5, 3), D(8, 1), E(7, 4), F(–2, 3), G(–4, 2),
H(–5, 4), I(–7, 3), J(–2, –4), K(–8, –3), L(–4, –2), M(2, –2), N(5, –4)**

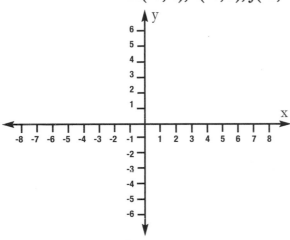

b) On the set of axes below, draw and name the lines, x = 3, y = 1 and x = –2.

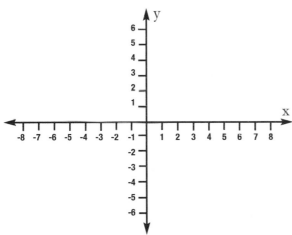

c) On the set of axes below, draw and name the lines, y = x and y = –x.

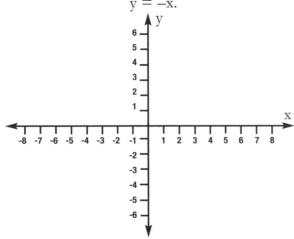

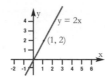

On a line represented by the equation y = 2x the y coordinate is double the x coordinate. For example, where x = 1, y = 2; where x = 2, y = 4.

So an equation shows the relationship between the x and y coordinates. When y = 5x, each y coordinate is 5 times the x coordinate (1, 5) (2, 10) etc.

For example, if the points (1, 3) (2, 6) and (–1, –3) are all on the same line, what is the equation of that line?
The y coordinate is three times the x coordinate, therefore y = 3x.

If the points (–2, –1) (1, $^1/_2$) (2, 1) (4, 2) are on a line, the y coordinate is half the x coordinate, therefore y = $^1/_2$x.
All these points can be plotted to show the lines:

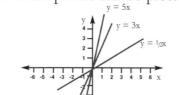

SLOPES AND GRADIENTS

The GRADIENT SLOPE (how much a slope rises or falls compared to how far along the horizontal you go) of a line is greater the larger the CO-EFFICIENT (the number in front of a letter) is. For example, y = 5x has a steeper gradient than y = $^1/_2$x (see diagram above).

The gradient of PARALLEL LINES (the co-efficient of x) is the same. For example, y = 2x and y = 2x + 3 are parallel lines. To plot these lines, first draw up a table for each:

y = 2x

x	–1	0	1
y	–2	0	2

y = 2x + 3

x	–1	0	1
y	1	3	5

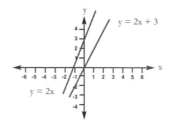

Draw the line y = 2x on a set of axes, and find the y co-ordinates of the points on the line that have x co-ordinates of:

a) 3   y = ☐

b) –2   y = ☐

c) 0   y = ☐

On the same axes draw and name the line y = –3x, and find the y co-ordinates of the points on the line that have x co-ordinates of:

d) 1   y = ☐

e) –1   y = ☐

f) –2   y = ☐

g) 0   y = ☐

Draw a set of axes:

h) If the equation of a line is y = 2x + 1, complete the table and draw the line.

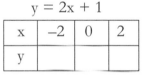

y = 2x + 1			
x	–2	0	2
y			

i) Where does it cross the y-axis?   y = ☐

j) What is the gradient of the line?   = ☐

k) Make up the equation of a line that would be parallel to the line y = 2x + 1.   ....

l) Make up a table and draw the line y = 3x + 2.

m) Where does it cross the y-axis?   y = ☐

n) What is the gradient?   = ☐

o) Make up the equation of a line that would be parallel to y = 3x + 2.   ....

If we have two equations such as $x + y = 5$ and $3x + y = 7$, a value of x and y will solve both equations simultaneously.

SIMULTANEOUS EQUATIONS – GRAPHS

To solve these equations, first draw them on the same graph, and where the graphs cross, the x and y co-ordinates solve both equations.

SUM 1 **Solve** $y = 5 - x$ $y = 7 - 3x$

METHOD $y = 5 - x$

x	−1	0	1	2
5−x	5+1	5−0	5−1	5−2
y	6	5	4	3

Step 1 Write out the equations.

Step 2 Draw up a table for each.

Step 3 Plot the co-ordinates on a graph and the points where they intersect will solve the equations.

$y = 7 - 3x$

x	−1	0	1	2
7−3x	7+3	7−0	7−3	7−6
y	10	7	4	1

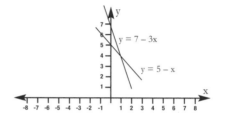

ANSWER **The co-ordinates of the intersection are $x = 1$, $y = 4$**

SIMULTANEOUS EQUATIONS – ALGEBRA

SUM 1 **Solve** $x + y = 5$ $3x + y = 7$

METHOD
$$\begin{aligned}
1.\ 3x + y &= 7 \\
2.\ x + y &= 5 \\
2x &= 2 \\
x &= 1 \\
x + y &= 5 \\
1 + y &= 5 \\
y &= 5 - 1 \\
y &= 4
\end{aligned}$$

Step 1 Write out the 2 equations with x below x as shown.

Step 2 Subtract equation 2 from equation 1 to allow y to disappear.

Step 3 Now work out the equation to find $x = 1$.

Step 4 Substitute 1 for x in equation 2.

Now you know the value of x, you can use it in the second equation. So $1 + y = 5$. In order to find y you must take the 1 to the other side and change its job. You can now find y.

ANSWER $x = 1$, $y = 4$

To check this is correct, place the new values of x and y into equation 1.
So $3x + y = 7$ (where $x = 1$ and $y = 4$)
$3 + 4 = 7$.

• If the signs are different, add the equations.

SUM 2 **Solve** $2x + y = 5$ $3x - y = 5$

METHOD
$$\begin{aligned}
1.\ 2x + y &= 5 \\
2.\ 3x - y &= 5 \\
5x &= 10 \\
x &= 2 \\
2x + y &= 5 \\
4 + y &= 5 \\
y &= 1
\end{aligned}$$

Use the same steps as above, but remember to add the two equations.

ANSWER $x = 2$, $y = 1$

Check these values in equation 2 ($6 - 1 = 5$).

Complete the TABLE for each equation, then draw the lines on a set of axes to find the solutions to these pairs of equations:

a) $y = 5 - 2x$ $y = 3 - x$

x			
y			

x			
y			

x = ☐   y = ☐

Without drawing a graph, solve these simultaneous equations ALGEBRAICALLY:

b) $3x - y = 9$
$2x - y = 2$

x = ☐   y = ☐

c) $2x + 2y = 14$
$2x + y = 9$

x = ☐   y = ☐

d) $7x - y = 5$
$3x - y = 1$

x = ☐   y = ☐

TEACHER'S TIP

It is necessary to make one of the letters disappear in order to find the value of the other. It does not matter if you find x or y first.

A distance/time graph is a diagram that shows precisely how distance and time relate to each other and allows us to determine speed.

For example, the graph below shows that in 3 hours someone walked 150 miles at a constant speed of 50mph. (After 1 hour, 50 miles, after 2 hours, 100 miles, after 3 hours, 150 miles etc.)

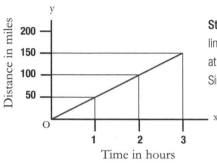

Step 1 Go one hour along the horizontal axis, go up to the line of the graph, then across to the vertical axis and arrive at 50 miles.
Similarly with 2 hours = 100 miles.

DRAWING A TRAVEL GRAPH

SUM 1 If the Jones family cycled at 30km/h, draw a graph to show that after 1 hour they had travelled 30km, after 2 hours, 60km and after 3 hours, 90km etc.

METHOD

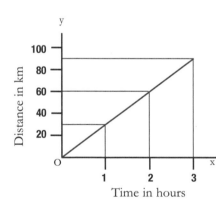

Step 1 Draw the graph with the time along the horizontal axis and the distance along the vertical axis.
Step 2 Find a suitable scale, for example 1cm to represent 10km and 2cm to represent 1hour.
Step 3 Plot the point which shows that in 1 hour the Jones's have cycled 30km. Join this point to the origin and draw the straight line, through the points as shown (left).

FORMULA
Speed is found in the same way as a gradient (see page 62).

$$\frac{\text{difference on y axis}}{\text{difference on x axis}} = \frac{90}{3} = 30\text{km/h}$$

distance = speed x time,
For example 30km/h x 2 = 60km

TEST 31

The following graphs **a) – d)** show four different journeys. For each journey find:

(i) time taken

(ii) speed

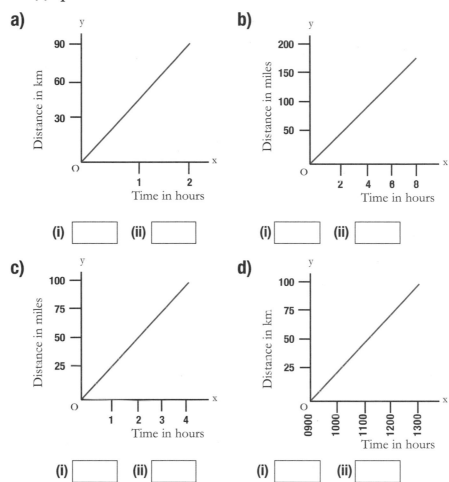

a)

(i) [ ]   (ii) [ ]

b)

(i) [ ]   (ii) [ ]

c)

(i) [ ]   (ii) [ ]

d)

(i) [ ]   (ii) [ ]

For **e)** and **f)** draw travel graphs to show the journey and find the speed:

e) 100km in $2^1/_2$ hours (use 1cm to represent 1 hour, and 2cm to represent 25km).

f) I left York at 10.47 to travel the 315 miles to Aberdeen. I arrived at 15.17.

TEACHER'S TIP

Always put the time along the horizontal axis and distance on the vertical axis.

LINEAR AND QUADRATIC EQUATIONS

Equations such as $x + 2 = 4$ are called linear equations as they contain x, the unknown, to a power of one only. Equations to a power of two or more are called quadratic equations and are more difficult to solve.

TRIAL AND IMPROVEMENT

Trial and improvement is a method that will help you solve these equations. The concept is to estimate a solution – using a calculator – and then improve on this estimation until sufficiently close to a solution.

SUM 1 $x^2 - 3x = 9$

Find the value of x to the nearest 1 decimal place

METHOD $x^2 - 3x = 9$

Step 1 Re-arrange the equation so that only terms containing x are on one side.

Step 2 Try substituting different values for x in the left hand side and compare the result with 9.

Try x = 4: When x = 4, $x^2 - 3x = 16 - 12 = 4$	Too small
Try x = 5: When x = 5, $x^2 - 3x = 25 - 15 = 10$	Too big, but closer
Try x = 4.5: When x = 4.5, $x^2 - 3x = 20.25 - 13.5 = 6.75$	Too small
Try x = 4.8: When x = 4.8, $x^2 - 3x = 23.04 - 14.4 = 8.64$	Too small, but close
Try x = 4.9: When x = 4.9, $x^2 - 3x = 24.01 - 14.7 = 9.31$	Too big, but close
Try x = 4.85: When x = 4.85, $x^2 - 3x = 23.5225 - 14.55 = 8.9725$	Too small, but VERY close

ANSWER The solution lies somewhere between 4.85 and 4.9 and as you were asked to find a solution to 1 decimal place, we give the nearest solution as: **x = 4.9 correct to one decimal place.**

SUM 2 **Use trial and improvement to find to one decimal place, the number for which: number + cube of number = 100**

METHOD $x + x^3 = 100$

$5^3 = 125$ and $4^3 = 64$

Step 1 Write out an equation, letting x be the unknown number.

Step 2 Try some values for x in the left hand side and compare the result with 100. As you may know $5^3 = 125$ and $4^3 = 64$. You will need to start somewhere between the two – perhaps 4.5.

Try x = 4.5: When x = 4.5, $x + x^3 = 4.5 + 91.125 = 95.625$	Too small
Try x = 4.6: When x = 4.6, $x + x^3 = 4.6 + 97.336 = 101.936$	Too big, but closer

ANSWER As 4.6 gives an answer closer to 100 (101.936) than 4.5 (95.625), we give the nearest solution as: **x = 4.6 to one decimal place.**

Using TRIAL AND IMPROVEMENT find the solutions to one decimal place:

a) $x^2 + x = 50$

$x = \boxed{}$ to 1 decimal place

b) $x^3 - x = 50$

$x = \boxed{}$ to 1 decimal place

c) $x + \dfrac{1}{x} = 7$

$x = \boxed{}$ to 1 decimal place

d) $x^4 = 14$

$x = \boxed{}$ to 1 decimal place

e) A number multiplied by itself equals 7 times the number. What is the number?

$x = \boxed{}$ to 1 decimal place

SPACE, SHAPE AND MEASURES

There are several facts about angles that you need to know:

Angles AT A POINT = 360°.
360° is called a complete revolution.

Angles on a STRAIGHT LINE add up to 180°.

A line that meets another at 90° is said to be perpendicular to the other line.
The angle is called a RIGHT ANGLE.

When two straight lines cross, the angles opposite each other are said to be VERTICALLY OPPOSITE angles.
They are equal, i.e. a = c, b = d.

An ACUTE ANGLE is less than 90°.

An OBTUSE ANGLE is greater than 90°, but less than 180°.

A REFLEX ANGLE is greater than 180°, but less than 360°.

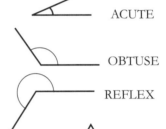

Angles in a triangle add up to 180°. (a + b + c = 180°)

ESTIMATING THE SIZE OF ANGLES

Using acute, obtuse, reflex and remembering 90°, 180° and 270°, it is possible to become used to estimating the size of angles.

PARALLEL LINES

When a TRANSVERSAL (line) cuts a pair of parallel lines, the following is true:

CORRESPONDING ANGLES are equal.

ALTERNATE ANGLES are equal.

INTERIOR ANGLES are supplementary i.e. they = 180°.

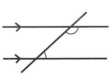

a) What do the angles on a straight line add up to? = [ ]

b) If one line is perpendicular to another, what size is the angle between them? = [ ]

c) What is the name given to an angle of 125°?

d) Estimate the size of angle x.

x = [ ]

e) Estimate the size of angle y.

y = [ ]

f) What size is angle z?

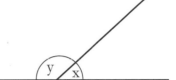

z = [ ]

Complete:

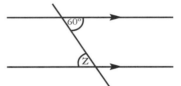

g) g = [ ]

h) h = [ ]

i) i = [ ]

j) j = [ ]

k) k = [ ]

l) Draw freehand an acute angle.

In this triangle a + b + c = 180º
On the straight line d + c = 180º
It follows that if we take c
away from both, then a + b = d

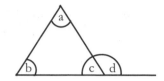

RULE: The exterior angle of a triangle (i.e. d) equals the sum of the two opposite interior angles (i.e. a + b).

An EQUILATERAL triangle has
3 equal sides and 3 equal angles –
$\frac{180}{3}$ = 60º.

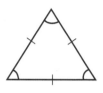

An ISOSCELES triangle has
2 equal sides and 2 equal angles.

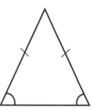

A SCALENE triangle does not have
any equal sides or angles.

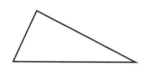

If two triangles have 3 equal sides (SSS), 2 equal angles and a corresponding side equal (AAS), two sides and the included angle equal (SAS), or a right angle, hypotenuse (the side of a triangle opposite to the right angle) and side equal (RHS) they are said to be CONGRUENT – exact copies of each other.

SSS

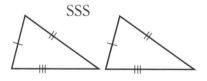

AAS

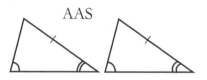

SAS

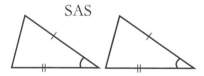

RHS

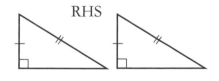

A QUADRILATERAL (a four-sided shape) with a diagonal drawn, may be thought of as two triangles. The sum of the angles of a quadrilateral is therefore 360º (2 x 180º).

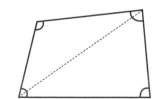

a) In this ISOSCELES TRIANGLE, angle a = 40°, write the sizes of (i) b, and (ii) c.

(i) b = ☐

(ii) c = ☐

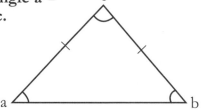

b) In this QUADRILATERAL, what is the size of d?

d = ☐

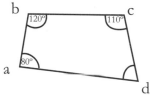

c) Find the size of angles (i) e, (ii) f, (iii) g:

(i) e = ☐

(ii) f = ☐

(iii) g = ☐

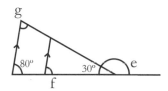

d) Are these triangles congruent?
If so, state the reason
(i.e. SSS, AAS, SAS or RHS)
Yes/No
Reason ....

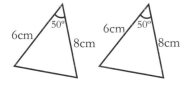

e) Using all the rules, find the following angles:

(i) i = ☐

(ii) j = ☐

(iii) k = ☐

(iv) l = ☐

(v) m = ☐

(vi) n = ☐

(vii) o = ☐

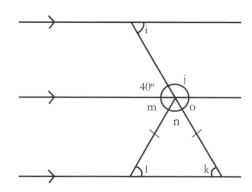

PROPERTIES OF QUADRILATERALS

A SQUARE is a quadrilateral with 4 equal sides and 4 right angles.

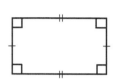

A RECTANGLE is a quadrilateral with opposite sides equal and 4 right angles.

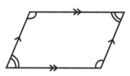

A PARALLELOGRAM is a quadrilateral with the opposite sides equal and parallel and the opposite angles equal.

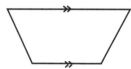

A TRAPEZIUM is a quadrilateral with only one pair of sides parallel, but not equal.

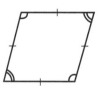

A RHOMBUS is a quadrilateral with 4 equal sides and pairs of opposite angles (2 obtuse and 2 acute).

A KITE is a quadrilateral made up of a pair of congruent SCALENE triangles.

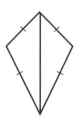

FORMULAE
The area of a rectangle is l x b = lb (length x breadth).
The area of a parallelogram is ba x h (base x vertical height).
The area of a triangle is half the area of a parallelogram = ½ ba x h.

How many EQUAL SIDES has:

a) a square?   = ☐

b) a trapezium? = ☐

c) a rhombus?   = ☐

d) Find the area of this square:

Area = ☐

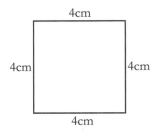

4cm

4cm   4cm

4cm

e) Find the AREA of this triangle:

Area = ☐

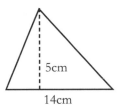

5cm

14cm

f) Find the AREA of this kite: .

Area = ☐

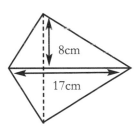

8cm

17cm

g) Find the AREA of this parallelogram:

Arca = ☐

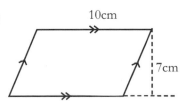

10cm

7cm

h) Using the formula for the area of a rectangle and triangle, find the AREA of this shape.

Area = ☐

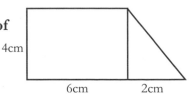

4cm

6cm   2cm

A POLYGON is a plane (flat) shape with any number of sides. The sum of the exterior angles of any polygon is always 360°.

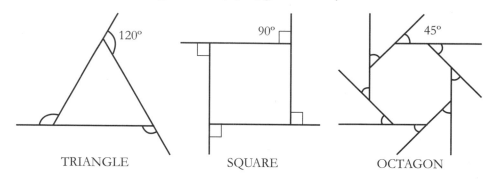

TRIANGLE   SQUARE   OCTAGON

RULE: For a regular polygon with 'n' sides, the size of each exterior angle $= \dfrac{360^0}{n}$.

Consider a regular hexagon. At each vertex (corner) there is an interior and exterior angle whose sum is 180° (angles on a straight line – see page 70). This means that the sum of the interior and exterior angles of a hexagon equals 6 x 180°. We have, however, found that the sum of the exterior angles of every polygon is 360°. Therefore, the sum of the interior angles of a hexagon is (6 x 180) – 360°. This formula works for the sum of the interior angles of an octagon:
i.e. (8 x 180) – 360°.

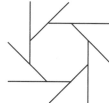

FORMULA
The following is true for all polygons of 'n' sides: The sum of the interior angles = (n x 180) – 360^0 or 180(n – 2).

SUM 1   **Find the sum of the interior angles of an octagon**

METHOD

180(n – 2)
180(8 – 2)
= 180 x 6
= 1080

Step 1 Use the formula to find the sum of the interior angles of a polygon (see FORMULA box above).
Step 2 Rewrite the formula, substituting 'n' for the number of sides of the required polygon (octagon = 8).
Step 3 Work out the sum.

ANSWER   **1080° (each interior angle in a regular octagon is $\dfrac{1080}{8} = 135°$)**

a) Find the sum of the interior angles of a pentagon.   = [   ]

b) Find the size of one interior angle of a pentagon.   = [   ]

c) Construct, using your protractor, a regular pentagon with sides 2cm long.

d) Find the size of each interior angle of a twelve-sided regular polygon.   = [   ]

Find the size of each angle marked in the diagrams e and f:

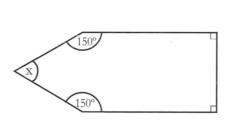

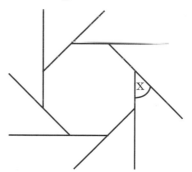

e) x = [   ]   **f)** x = [   ]

Pythagoras was a Greek mathematician who lived for some time in Egypt. There he studied with priests and learned men who had studied texts and methods from India. From this study Pythagoras made a discovery which has come to be known as PYTHAGORAS' THEOREM.

RULE: The square on the hypotenuse of a right-angled triangle equals the sum of the squares on the other two sides. NOTE: It only applies to a right-angled triangle. If we draw squares on the two sides of a right-angled triangle and cut them up into strips, we would find that they would cover exactly the square on the hypotenuse.

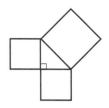

SUM 1 **In triangle ABC, AB = 4cm, AC = 3cm. Find the length of BC**

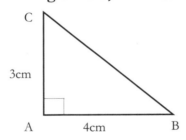

METHOD

$$BC^2 = AB^2 + AC^2$$
$$= 4^2 + 3^2$$
$$= 16 + 9$$
$$BC = \sqrt{25} = 5cm$$

Step 1 Apply Pythagoras' theorem – the square on the hypotenuse (BC) equals the sum of the squares on the other two sides (AB and AC).

Step 2 Work out the sum. $AB^2 = 4 \times 4 = 16$. $AC^2 = 3 \times 3 = 9$. $BC^2 = 16 + 9 = 25$.

Step 3 This is BC^2. To find BC find the square root of 25.

• When you are given the length of the hypotenuse and want to find the length of another side, you will need to use subtraction.

SUM 2 **In triangle XYZ, XZ = 13cm, XY = 5cm. Find the length of YZ**

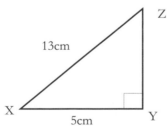

METHOD

$$YZ^2 = XZ^2 - XY^2$$
$$= 13^2 - 5^2$$
$$= 169 - 25 = 144$$
$$YZ = \sqrt{144} = 12cm$$

Step 1 Apply Pythagoras' theorem. Because you know the length of the hypotenuse, you use minus.

Step 2 Work out the sum – as above. REMEMBER, to find YZ, you will need to find the square root of 144.

a)

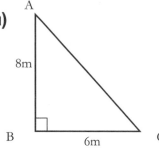

Find AC = [   ]

b)

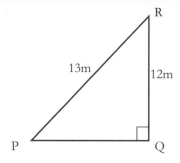

Find PQ = [   ]

c)

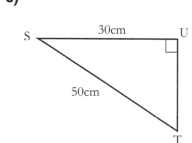

Find TU = [   ]

d)

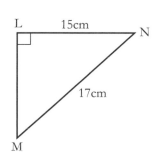

Find LM = [   ]

e)

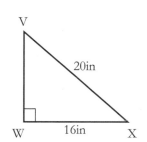

Find VW = [   ]

f)

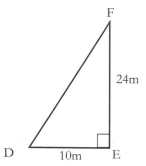

Find DF = [   ]

TEACHER'S TIP

Remember, the hypotenuse is always the side opposite the right angle.

We heave a sigh of relief to be able to use calculators when squaring, but a few points need watching:

1) Above the numbers on the calculator is a button, usually marked $\boxed{x^2}$. To square 17, enter 17 in the usual way and press $\boxed{x^2}$. Immediately the answer 289 shows.

2) To find AC when $AC^2 = 193$, we find the square root button $\boxed{\sqrt{}}$. Usually (read your calculator instructions to verify) $\sqrt{193}$ is found by first entering $\boxed{1}\boxed{9}\boxed{3}$ then $\boxed{\sqrt{}}$ then $\boxed{=}$. The display shows 13.8924439894.

3) When we have come to the end of our calculation (and not before) we round off to the number of decimal places asked. In this case, if it is to one decimal place, the answer is given as 13.9.

SUM 1 **Find XY, giving the length to one decimal place (use a calculator).**

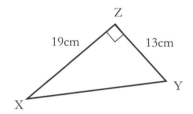

METHOD

$$XY^2 = XZ^2 + YZ^2$$
$$= 19^2 + 13^2$$
$$= 361 + 169$$
$$= 530$$
$$XY = \sqrt{530}$$
$$= 23.02172887\text{cm}$$

Step 1 Apply Pythagoras' theorem – the square on the hypotenuse (XY) equals the sum of the squares on the other two sides (XZ and YZ).

Step 2 Work out the sum $XZ^2 + YZ^2$.

Step 3 This gives you XY^2. To find XY you will need to find the square root of 530 – you can use your calculator.

ANSWER **23.0cm (to one decimal place)**

SUM 2 **Find BC, giving the length to one decimal place**

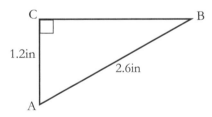

METHOD

$$BC^2 = AB^2 - AC^2$$
$$= 2.6^2 - 1.2^2$$
$$= 6.76 - 1.44$$
$$= 5.32$$
$$BC = \sqrt{532}$$
$$= 2.306512519\text{in}$$

NOTE: Use the same steps as above, but remember because you know the length of the hypotenuse you must minus to work out the sum.

ANSWER **2.3in (to one decimal place)**

Find all the answers to one decimal place:

a) **Find BC**

BC = ☐

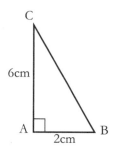

b) **Find YZ**

YZ = ☐

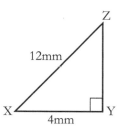

c) **Find SR**

SR = ☐

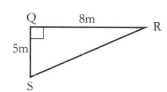

d) **Find DF**

DF = ☐

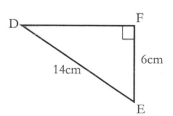

e) **Find HI**

HI = ☐

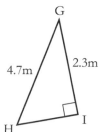

f) **Find LM**

LM = ☐

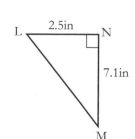

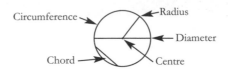

The curved line which is the outline of the circle is called the CIRCUMFERENCE (*circum* = round, *ferre* = carry). Every point on the circumference is equidistant from the centre. This distance is called the RADIUS. A straight line joining any two points on the circumference is called a CHORD. Any chord passing through the centre is a DIAMETER (above).

Minor Arc, AB

Major Arc, AB

Any part of the circumference is called an arc. If the arc is less than half the circumference, it is a MINOR ARC, if greater a MAJOR ARC.

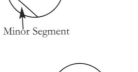

Major Segment

Minor Segment

A chord divides a circle into two SEGMENTS. If a segment is exactly half a circle, it is a SEMI-CIRCLE. If it is less, it is a MINOR SEGMENT, if more a MAJOR SEGMENT.

Sector

When two radii and an arc enclose a 'slice' of a circle, this area is called a SECTOR.

• The circumference of a circle can be found using $C = 2\pi r$.

SUM 1   **Find the circumference, where the radius of a circle is 2cm**

METHOD

$C = 2\pi r$

   $= 2 \times 3.142 \times 2$

   $= 4 \times 3.142$

   $= 12.568$cm

Step 1 Write out the formula: $C = 2\pi r$.

Step 2 Rewrite the sum, replacing the letters with numbers.

Remember $\pi = 3.142$ and the radius is 2cm.

Step 3 Work out the sum: $4 \times 3.142 = 12.568$.

• Where the diameter is known, use $C = \pi d$.

SUM 2   **Find the circumference, where the diameter of a circle is 3cm**

METHOD

$C = \pi d$

   $= 3.142 \times 3$

   $= 9.426$cm

Step 1 Write out the formula: $C = \pi d$.

Step 2 Rewrite the sum, replacing the letters with numbers.

Step 3 Work out the sum: $3 \times 3.142 = 9.426$.

• The area of a circle can be found using $A = \pi r^2$.

SUM 3   **If the radius of a circle is 2cm, find its area**

METHOD

$A = \pi r^2$

$A = 3.142 \times 2 \times 2$

   $= 3.142 \times 4$

   $= 12.5682$cm

Step 1 Write out the formula: $A = \pi r^2$

Step 2 Rewrite the sum, using figures. Remember,

$\pi = 3.142$ and the radius is 2.

a) Name five chords in this circle. Write D beside the one that is a diameter.

1 = ...

2 = ...

3 = ...

4 = ...

5 = ...

b) Shade the minor segment.

c) Highlight the major arc.

d) If radius OR = 4cm, find the circumference of the circle.

Circumference = ☐

e) If radius XY = 3cm, find the area of the circle.

Area = ☐

f) If diameter PQ = 5cm, find the circumference of the circle.

Circumference = ☐

FORMULAE
- The circumference can be found using the formula $C = 2 \pi r$.
- The area of a circle can be found using the formula $A = \pi r^2$.

$\pi = 3.142$ OR $\dfrac{22}{7}$ approximately.

In the chapter on polygons, we looked at areas of two-dimensional shapes i.e. plane figures. The amount of space a solid takes up is called volume. Volume is measured in cubed units (cm^3, ft^3 etc).

CUBOIDS AND PRISMS

> **FORMULAE**
> • The formula for the volume of a cuboid is: $v = l \times b \times h$ (length x breadth x height).
> • The formula for the volume of a prism is: v = area of cross-section x length.
> • The formula for the area of a circle is $A = \pi r^2$ (see page 82).

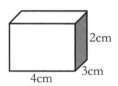

SUM 1   **Find the volume of a cuboid where its length is 4cm, breadth is 3cm, height is 2cm**

METHOD   Volume, $v = l \times b \times h$
             $= 4 \times 3 \times 2$

ANSWER   **24cm³**

Step 1 Write out the formula for the volume of a cuboid l x b x h

Step 2 Replace the letters with measurements and work out. Remember volume is measured in cubed units.

• A prism is like a cuboid but has an end that is not a square or rectangle.

TRIANGULAR PRISM

PLAN AND ELEVATION

Using the triangular prism above as an example:

The PLAN view
Looking from above

FRONT ELEVATION
Looking from front

SIDE ELEVATION
Looking from side

NETS

• A net is a two-dimensional shape, which can be folded to make the solid. For example,

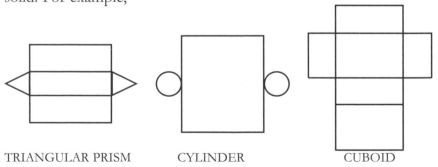

TRIANGULAR PRISM   CYLINDER   CUBOID

Draw these shapes on a piece of paper; cut them out and fold them up to see the solid shapes they make.

Find the VOLUME of the following two shapes:

a)

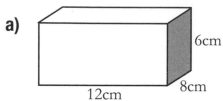

6cm

8cm

12cm

Volume =

b)

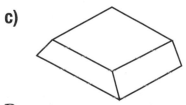

0.3m

0.5m

0.8m

Volume =

c)

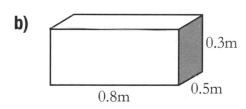

Draw
I) plan   **ii) front elevation**   **iii) side elevation**

d) Square-based pyramid

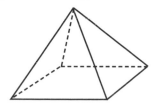

Draw
i) plan   **ii) front elevation**   **iii) side elevation**

When we wish to find our bearings, we do so in relation to a fixed reference. That is to the direction NORTH.
For example,

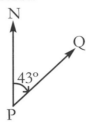

Find the bearing of Q from P.
The word FROM is important. The point following FROM (in this case P) is where we draw the line in the direction NORTH. We join the point P to Q and measure the angle. In this case, the bearing Q FROM P is 043°.

NOTE – Always measure the angle of the bearing CLOCKWISE from NORTH.

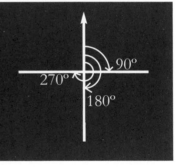

TEACHER'S TIP
• Knowing that 90°, 180° and 270° look like this allows you to estimate the bearing before you measure or calculate it exactly.

SUM 1   **The bearing of B from A is 132°. What is the bearing of A from B?**

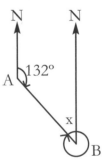

METHOD   Angle x = 180 − 132° (interior angles of parallel lines)
        = 48°
Therefore the bearing of A FROM B
= 360° − 48°
= 312°

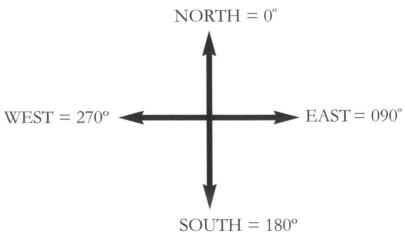

NORTH = 0°

WEST = 270°   EAST = 090°

SOUTH = 180°

Find the BEARING of B from A in each of the following diagrams:

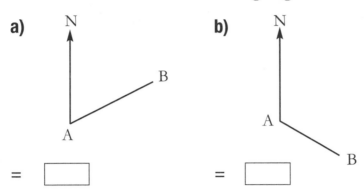

a)

= ☐

b)

= ☐

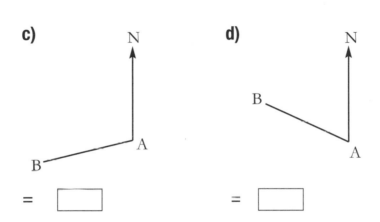

c)

= ☐

d)

= ☐

Draw a diagram to represent the following:

e) A ship sails 10 miles from A on a bearing of 110° to B. It then sails 5 miles to C on a bearing of 75°.
(Use 0.5cm to represent 1 mile).

f) A man walks 7 miles from A on a bearing of 250° to B. From B he walks 3 miles east to C.

g) The bearing of B from A is 285°. What is the bearing of A from B? (You may want to draw a diagram to help you.)

TEACHER'S TIP
All lines pointing NORTH are parallel.

A TRANSFORMATION is a process that changes the position of an object. A TRANSLATION moves the object forwards or backwards, up or down. Movements forwards and upward are represented as POSITIVE. Movements backwards and downward are represented as NEGATIVE. This movement is written as a vector, the top number indicating movement on the x-axis, and the lower number, movement on the y-axis.

Example 1,   Example 2,   Example 3,

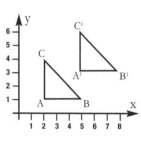

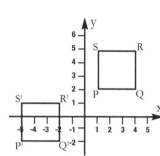

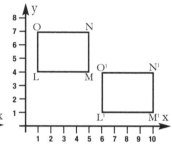

ABC has been translated to the image A^{1}B^{1}C^1 by moving 3 squares forwards and 2 upward, i.e. $\binom{3}{2}$

PQRS is mapped to P^{1}Q^{1}R^{1}S^1 by the translation described by the vector $\binom{-6}{-4}$

LMNO has been mapped to L^{1}M^{1}N^{1}O^1 by the translation $\binom{5}{-3}$

REFLECTION

In REFLECTIONS the object and the image together form a symmetrical shape and the MIRROR line is the axis of symmetry.

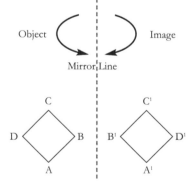

A is the same distance to the left of the mirror line as A^1 is to the right of the mirror line etc.

• If you are given a shape and asked to reflect it in a mirror line, take each point and measure its vertical distance to the mirror line. Measure the same distance on the other side of the mirror line and plot the point. Repeat for all points and plot the reflected shape.

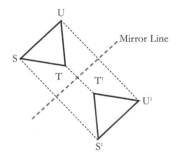

Describe whether each is a TRANSLATION or REFLECTION and give the vector or draw the mirror line:

a)

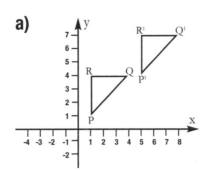

= ....

b)

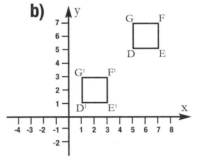

= ....

c)

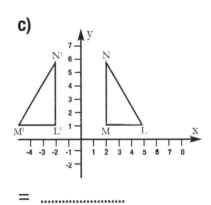

= ....

d)

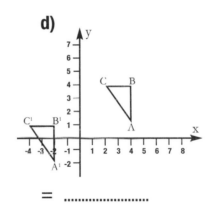

= ....

e) Reflect in the mirror line.

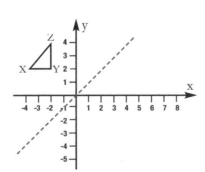

f) Map triangle FGH to F¹G¹H¹ using the vector $\binom{6}{5}$. Draw F¹G¹H¹.

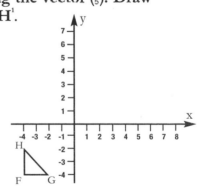

To transform ABC to $A^1B^1C^1$, we have rotated the triangle through $90°$ clockwise about the point B. We could also say that we rotated the triangle through $270°$ anticlockwise about B.

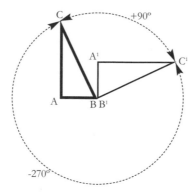

There are three points to make clear in a rotation:

1. The number of degrees of rotation.
2. The direction of rotation, clockwise or anticlockwise.
3. The centre of rotation.

Example 1,

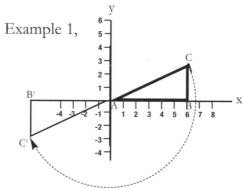

ABC is rotated through $180°$ clockwise about the centre $(0, 0)$.

Example 2,

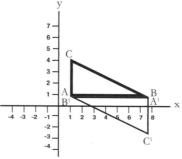

ABC is rotated $180°$ through $(4, 1)$.

Example 3,

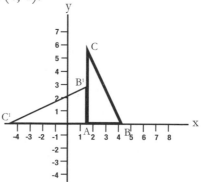

ABC is rotated $90°$ anticlockwise through $(1, 0)$.

Describe the ROTATION of triangle ABC to A¹B¹C¹, remembering to mention the 3 points:

a)

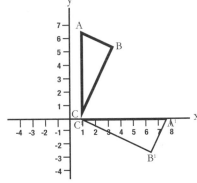

ABC = ...

b)

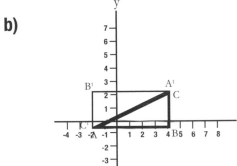

ABC = ...

c)

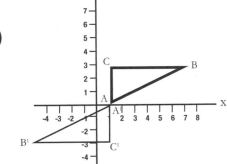

ABC = ...

44. ENLARGEMENTS

An ENLARGEMENT changes the size (and probably the position) of an object. The amount by which the lengths are changed is called the SCALE FACTOR.

A scale factor of 2 makes all the lengths twice as long. A scale factor of $^1/_2$ makes the lengths half as long. All enlargements take place from a centre of enlargement. There are two things to make clear in an enlargement: **1)** scale factor, **2)** centre of enlargement.

Example 1,

Example 2,   O = centre of enlargement

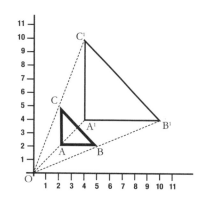

Triangle ABC is enlarged by a scale factor of 2, centre about the origin O.
$(OA^1 = 2 \times OA, OB^1 = 2 \times OB, OC^1 = 2 \times OC)$

Triangle XYZ is enlarged by a scale factor of $^1/_2$, centre about the origin O.
$(OX^1 = {^1/_2} OX, OY^1 = {^1/_2} OY, OZ^1 = {^1/_2} OZ)$

Example 3,

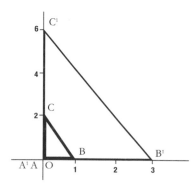

Triangle ABC is enlarged by scale factor 3, centre about the origin O.
$OA^1 = 3 \times OA$ (Note A, A^1 and O are the same point).
$OB^1 = 3 \times OB$
$OC^1 = 3 \times OC$

ENLARGE TRIANGLES ABC in each of the following:

a)

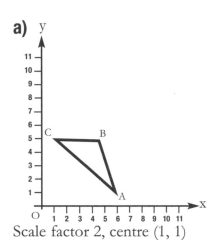

Scale factor 2, centre (1, 1)

b)

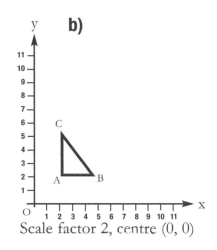

Scale factor 2, centre (0, 0)

c) Describe with all the necessary detailed points the TRANSFORMATION of triangle ABC to:

(i) $A^1B^1C^1$

= ....

(ii) $A^2B^2C^2$

= ....

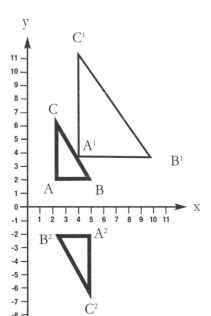

TEACHER'S TIP

Angles stay the same when enlarging.

TO DRAW AN EQUILATERAL TRIANGLE

SUM 1 Construct an equilateral triangle of side 2 inches

METHOD

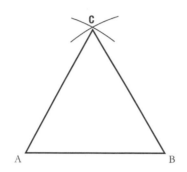

Step 1 Draw the line AB two inches long — make sure you leave enough room on the page to draw the lines above.

Step 2 Stretch the compasses to give a radius of 2 inches long. With the centre at A, draw an arc above AB.

Step 3 With the same radius and centre at B, draw another arc which cuts the first one at C.

Step 4 Join AC and BC where the arcs cross. The resulting triangle will be equilateral.

TO BISECT A LINE PERPENDICULARLY

SUM 2 Bisect a line perpendicularly

METHOD

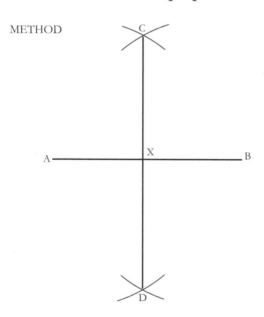

Step 1 Leaving plenty of room for construction lines, draw a line AB.

Step 2 Stretch the compasses to more than half the length of AB.

Step 3 With the centre at A, draw arcs above and below AB.

Step 4 With the centre at B and using the same radius, draw arcs above and below AB which cut the first two arcs at C and D.

Step 5 Join CD, cutting AB at X. CD is the perpendicular bisector of AB.

TEACHER'S TIP

Remember, a perpendicular is a line which meets or crosses another line at a right angle.

TEST 45

a) Draw an EQUILATERAL TRIANGLE of side 3cm.

b) Draw a line AB (3.5cm) and bisect it PERPENDICULARLY.

c) Draw an EQUILATERAL TRIANGLE of side 4cm.

TEACHER'S TIP

Ensure that the point of the compasses and sharp point of the pencil almost touch each other when held vertically with the points resting on a surface.

BISECTING AN ANGLE

SUM 1 Bisect a given angle, BAC

METHOD

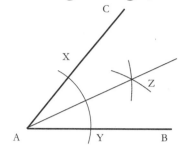

Step 1 With centre A and radius about 1/2 of AB draw an arc cutting AC and AB at X and Y.

Step 2 With centre X and a similar radius draw an arc lying between AB and AC. With exactly the same radius and centre Y, draw an arc to cut the first arc at Z.

Step 3 Join AZ. AZ bisects angle BAC.

TO DRAW A PERPENDICULAR

SUM 1 Draw a perpendicular from a point to a given line (AB). Let x be the point

METHOD

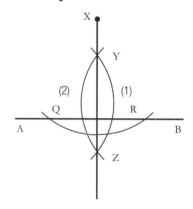

Step 1 With centre x and a radius which will pass through AB twice, draw an arc and let the points where it cuts AB be Q and R.

Step 2 With centre Q and radius a little greater than QR, draw a large arc (1).

Step 3 With the same radius and centre R draw another arc (2), cutting the previous one at Y and Z.

Step 4 Join XYZ. The line XYZ is perpendicular to AB.

TO DRAW A PERPENDICULAR FROM A POINT

SUM 1 Draw a perpendicular from a point on a given line (AC)

The perpendicular to the straight line will be at point A.

METHOD

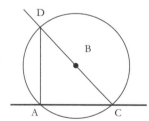

Step 1 Choose a point B, above the line so that with radius AB and centre B a circle drawn will cut the straight line at C.

Step 2 Join CB and extend it to D to make a diameter.

Step 3 Join AD. AD is the perpendicular to AC at A. (The angle DAC = 90° and is a right-angle in a semi-circle.)

a) Bisect PQR.

P

Q   R

b) Draw a **PERPENDICULAR** from L to MN.

• L

M   N

c) Draw a **PERPENDICULAR** from P.

P

A locus (from the Latin word meaning place) is the path traced out by a single moving point under certain rules. A locus may encompass a whole area or volume.

If a goat is tethered to a post the furthest it could go from the post would be the length of the rope, and the area it could graze would be a circle of this radius.

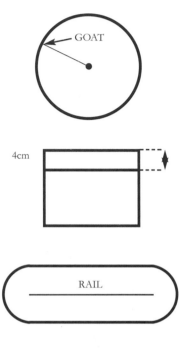

If we consider a point on this page, which moves so that it is always 4cm from the top of the page, this is a line parallel to the top of the page, 4cm from it.

If, however, we consider a horse on a sliding tether which was joined to a rail, this means that it could move along the rail and round each end and along the other side. The locus of the greatest distance from the rail is a pair of parallel lines on each side of the rail with a pair of semi-circles, one at each end of the lines.

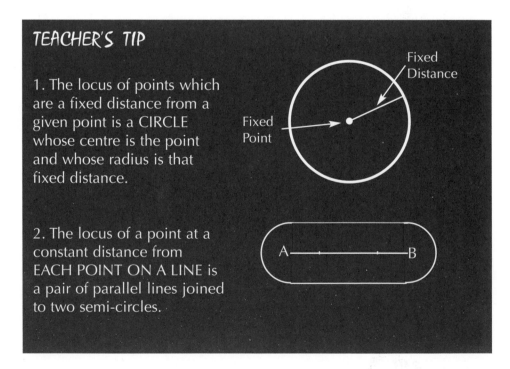

TEACHER'S TIP

1. The locus of points which are a fixed distance from a given point is a CIRCLE whose centre is the point and whose radius is that fixed distance.

2. The locus of a point at a constant distance from EACH POINT ON A LINE is a pair of parallel lines joined to two semi-circles.

a) Draw the LOCUS of the tip of the minute hand of a clock as it sweeps through one hour.

b) Draw the LOCUS (approximately) of a satellite orbiting the earth.

c) Draw the LOCUS of a point, which is exactly 1cm from ALL of this line.

X ————————————————— Y

Before we are able to draw graphs or charts to illustrate statistics we need to collect the information. We do this by SAMPLING, i.e. asking only part of the whole population. Obviously, the more people in the sample, the more accurate will be the results. RANDOM SAMPLING means selecting perhaps every tenth (or other number) person in a group. STRATIFIED SAMPLING tries to take the same number of samples from each strata (or section) of a group. Strata can be grouped by age, gender etc.

Example of Questionnaire to test
'Do parents believe that there is enough sport at school?'

QUESTION 1
Did you enjoy sport in your youth?   YES
(This allows us to determine whether the parent   NO
appreciates sport)

QUESTION 2
Do you have children of school age?   YES
(This determines their increased interest in the   NO
subject)

QUESTION 3
To which age group do they belong?   5–10
(Answers could depend on the age of the children)   11–13
                                                            14–16
                                                            17–18

QUESTION 4
Do they do sport at school?   YES
(This determines if the parent knows about sport   NO
at school)

QUESTION 5
Which of these sports do they do?   Basketball
(This focuses attention on the subject)   Netball
                                                            Lacrosse
                                                            Hockey
                                                            Football
                                                            Rugby
                                                            Cricket
                                                            Athletics
                                                            Rowing
                                                            Swimming

QUESTION 6
Do you think that time for sport at school is: Too short
(This allows for a simple answer)   Just right
                                                            Too long

These questions focus the attention on SPORT and give a simple choice of answers.

Using five or six questions, design a QUESTIONNAIRE to collect data on each of the following:

a) The time people take over breakfast on weekdays.

b) Transport to school each day.

c) The interests of young teenagers, for a new shopping centre which would like to encourage them to shop there.

TEACHER'S TIP

Questions in a questionnaire need to be unambiguous. There should be few (10 at most) questions. Answers should be simple Yes/No, Too short/Too long/Just right etc. Questions should be unbiased, i.e. they should NOT be slanted to favour particular answers.

This is a list of the number of pets owned by thirty pupils in a class. Each figure represents the number of pets of one member of the class:

0	2	1	3	0	2	1	0	0	4
1	3	1	1	0	3	1	0	1	2
1	4	2	0	1	1	1	1	0	2

To use the numbers we need to group them. We may do this using a FREQUENCY TABLE. The 'frequency' tells us how often (or frequently) that number is in our list. We list the numbers and make a tally mark, /, for each one. Every fifth one we write horizontally to make for easy counting (////). We write the tally total in the frequency column. Lastly, we add up all the 'frequencies' to check that the total is the same number as we have members in the class.

This is the simple way to chart definite or **discrete** data.

Number of Pets	Tally	Frequency
0	//// ///	8
1	//// //// //	12
2	////	5
3	///	3
4	//	2
	Total	30

To chart CONTINUOUS DATA, we need to group it into classes, e.g. here are the heights of 72 pupils in a year group (in inches):

58	60	57	55	62	64	59	58	65	66	67	60
60	55	60	59	59	53	58	60	63	61	57	59
54	57	57	53	58	61	57	60	66	65	59	60
62	66	55	52	58	60	65	65	61	63	55	62
53	67	62	65	60	59	65	68	62	62	54	67
55	54	64	62	66	62	66	62	60	58	57	59

Taking h to represent the height of a pupil, a suitable grouping is: $50 \le h < 55$, $55 \le h < 60$, $60 \le h < 65$, $65 \le h < 70$. In a frequency table the information looks like this:

Group	Tally	Frequency
$50 \le h < 55$	//// //	7
$55 \le h < 60$	//// //// //// //// ////	24
$60 \le h < 65$	//// //// //// //// //// /	26
$65 \le h < 70$	//// //// ////	15
	Total	72

Draw a FREQUENCY TABLE of:

a) The **DISCRETE DATA** of shoe sizes for 24 seven-year-olds.

2	5	3	4	6	4	5	6
3	2	4	5	3	3	4	2
4	2	2	5	5	3	3	4

b) The **CONTINUOUS DATA** of tomato yield by 30 plants, in kg.

3	4	2	5	6	1	0	2	5	4	3	1	2	1	1
5	6	6	1	4	1	4	3	2	4	3	5	4	4	5

c) The ages of 40 men employed in a factory.

27	36	42	50	59	31	27	35	48	50
29	48	20	19	61	35	25	59	57	53
54	33	17	33	23	49	32	34	23	46
60	25	23	19	18	56	54	43	62	39

A PICTOGRAPH is a very simple way of representing data. For example, if 18 children had the shoe sizes shown in the frequency table below, a pictograph could represent this:

Shoe Size	No. of Children
2	3
3	4
4	6
5	5

The same frequency can be represented on a BAR CHART.
NB Frequency is the vertical axis.

The table may be represented on a VERTICAL LINE DIAGRAM, also called a 'stick graph', bar line chart or frequency bar diagram.

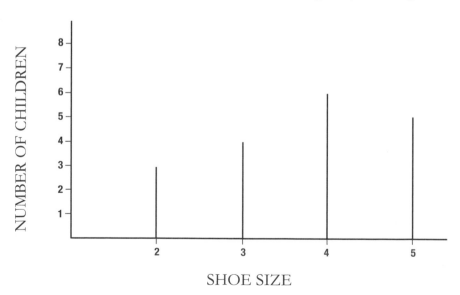

Draw **(i)** a PICTOGRAPH **(ii)** a BAR CHART **(iii)** a VERTICAL LINE DIAGRAM:

a) To represent the following table which illustrates the number of eggs a hen lays each day in one week.

Days of the Week	Number of Eggs
Monday	3
Tuesday	4
Wednesday	2
Thursday	3
Friday	2
Saturday	2
Sunday	4

(i)   **(ii)**

(iii)

b) To represent the number of goals scored by the local football team in five matches.

Match Number	1	2	3	4	5
Number of Goals	0	1	2	4	6

(i)   **(ii)**

(iii)

When illustrating CONTINUOUS DATA, the bars on a bar chart must touch each other (not necessary for discrete data). The dividing lines are drawn at the deciding value between the classes. The results of a maths test for 30 pupils are illustrated in the frequency table below:

25, 32, 37, 38, 39, 41, 43, 48, 50, 50, 51, 52, 52, 55, 56,
60, 61, 61, 65, 66, 66, 68, 72, 75, 78, 80, 81, 83, 88, 90.

Marks	Frequency
$0 < M \le 20$	0
$20 < M \le 40$	5
$40 < M \le 60$	11
$60 < M \le 80$	10
$80 < M \le 100$	4

As a FREQUENCY DIAGRAM: As a FREQUENCY POLYGON:

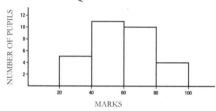 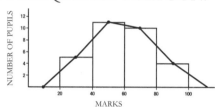

You mark up the centre of each bar and join them up with straight lines.

Or for a FREQUENCY POLYGON (without frequency diagram), we mark at midpoints imaginary bars at each end on the horizontal axis.

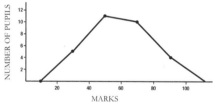

Do not forget that the point is marked at the centre of each class: i.e. for $20 < M \le 40$ plot the point above 30.

From the same data a STEM AND LEAF diagram can be made.

25, 32, 37, 38, 39, 41, 43, 48, 50, 50, 51, 52, 52, 55, 56,
60, 61, 61, 65, 66, 66, 68, 72, 75, 78, 80, 81, 83, 88, 90.

```
0  |
20 | 5 12 17 18 19
40 | 1 3 8 10 10 11 12 12 15 16
60 | 0 1 1 5 6 6 8 12 15 18
80 | 0 1 3 8 10
```

Step 1 Write down the lowest number in each class on the left-hand side of a vertical straight line.
Step 2 On the right-hand side of the line, opposite each class write, in ascending order, the number by which each mark is greater than the lowest number in the class. For example, an exam mark of 25 is written as 5 in the row of class 20. i.e. 20 * 5, 32 is written 20 * 12 and 60 is written 60 * 0.

When placed on its side the stem and leaf diagram has a shape similar to the frequency diagram or frequency polygon.

a) Here is a frequency table. Using its contents, draw a **FREQUENCY DIAGRAM** and, on top of the diagram, carefully construct a **FREQUENCY POLYGON**.

Salaries in a business Annual Payment	Number of Employees
$8,000 \leq p < 9,000$	8
$9,000 \leq p < 10,000$	12
$10,000 \leq p < 11,000$	15
$11,000 \leq p < 12,000$	11
$12,000 \leq p < 13,000$	4

b) This is a frequency table showing how many hours of television are watched by 30 children in a week. Make a **FREQUENCY DIAGRAM** and impose a **FREQUENCY POLYGON** on top of it.

Number of hours of television watched	Number of children
$0 \leq h < 2$	2
$2 \leq h < 4$	6
$4 \leq h < 6$	4
$6 \leq h < 8$	8
$8 \leq h < 10$	10

c) From this frequency table, draw a **FREQUENCY POLYGON** to illustrate heights of children in a class of pupils.

Heights (cm)	Frequency
$140 \leq h < 145$	3
$145 \leq h < 150$	8
$150 \leq h < 155$	12
$155 \leq h < 160$	15
$160 \leq h < 165$	2

d) In an English test, marked out of 50, the results were:

9, 11, 12, 20, 24, 28, 32, 33, 34, 36, 40, 42, 45, 45, 47, 48.

From this data construct a **STEM AND LEAF DIAGRAM**.

0	
10	
20	
30	
40	

PIE CHARTS represent information in a circle – hence the name 'pie'. The circle is cut into different sized sectors (see pages 82–83).

The angle (at the centre) of each sector shows the quantity represented by that sector. You can find out the size of all the angles using, as the basis of your calculations, the 'whole' = 360° (as angles at a point add up to 360°). Then multiply by the frequency.

The results of a transport survey show the number of people coming to school in different ways:

Transport	Frequency	As 120 pupils are represented by 360^0
		1 pupil will be represented by $360^0 \div 120^0 = 3^0$
Car	23	23 pupils will be represented by $3 \times 23 = 69^0$
Bus	17	17 pupils will be represented by $3 \times 17 = 51^0$
Train	25	25 pupils will be represented by $3 \times 25 = 75^0$
Bicycle	15	15 pupils will be represented by $3 \times 15 = 45^0$
Walk	40	40 pupils will be represented by $3 \times 40 = 120^0$
Total	120	Check the Total = 360°

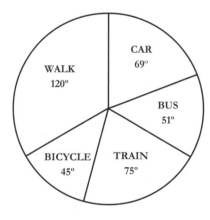

Step 1 Draw a circle and mark the centre clearly.
Step 2 Draw a radius.
Step 3 From the radius measure the angles.
Step 4 Draw the sectors and label them.

However, you may be given a pie chart and asked to work out how many pupils out of the total 120 travelled by bicycle.

$$\frac{45}{360_3} \times \frac{\cancel{120}^1}{1} = \frac{45}{3}$$

$$= 15 \text{ pupils}$$

Step 1 Measure the angles at the centre of the bicycle sector in the pie chart = 45°.
Step 2 Divide by 360° (the 'whole'). So divide 45 by 360 and multiply by $^{120}/_1$.
Step 3 Then cancel = $^{45}/_3$ = 15.

a) In a class of 36 pupils, 7 have black hair, 12 have fair hair, 1 has blond hair, 8 have brown hair, 2 have red hair and 6 have auburn hair. Calculate appropriate angles and draw a **PIE CHART** for the information.

b) In a park there are 60 trees. 20 are lime trees, 10 are sycamore, 9 are horse chestnut trees, 5 are beech, 8 are birch, 6 are oak and 2 are maples. With suitable calculations, draw a **PIE CHART** to represent this.

c) At an international event, the number of people to represent each nation is illustrated in the pie chart below. Work out how many there are per nationality, if there are 1080 people in all.

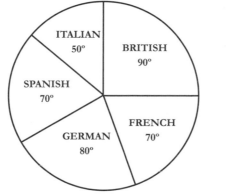

British   = ☐

French   = ☐

German   = ☐

Spanish   = ☐

Italian   = ☐

Scatter graphs are used to discover if there is a connection between two sets of data. This connection is called a CORRELATION.

Example 1,

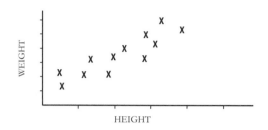

The graph above shows a POSITIVE correlation – as the height of a person increases, so their weight increases.

Example 2,

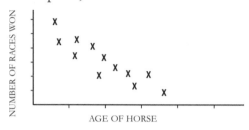

The graph above shows a NEGATIVE correlation – as the age of the horse increases, the number of races it wins decreases.

Example 3,

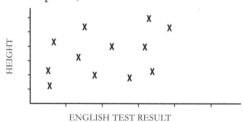

The graph above shows that the height of a person has NO correlation with English test results.

• If there is a correlation (positive or negative) a LINE OF BEST FIT is drawn so that we have roughly the same number of points on either side of it. The polarity of the gradient of the line of best fit is the same as that of the correlation:

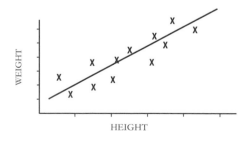 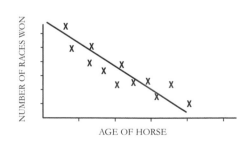

a) The table shows English and French test marks for 12 people. Draw a **SCATTER GRAPH**, plotting the points carefully. Draw a line of best fit and state if there is any correlation, and if there is, whether it is negative or positive.

ENGLISH MARK	70	30	40	65	80	55	48	67	73	45	59	69
FRENCH MARK	68	25	45	69	69	70	50	40	62	50	70	60

b) In an ice skating championship, 2 judges gave the following marks for 7 skaters. Illustrate these marks on a **SCATTER DIAGRAM**. Comment on the relationship between them.

JUDGE 1	7.7	8.1	7.9	8.0	9.0	7.4	8.5
JUDGE 2	6.9	7.9	7.8	8.1	8.9	7.6	7.6

c) Language students were given oral and written tests. Use a **SCATTER DIAGRAM** to find out if there is a relationship between the scores in the two tests.

Oral Test	20	10	14	7	16	8	7	6	14	8
Written Test	19	4	8	12	5	12	14	12	10	17

Averages are of three types, mean, mode and median. MEAN is what we usually think of as average i.e. the total sum of our data divided by the number of pieces of data.

For example, the mean of 1 1 2 3 3 4 4 4 5

is $\dfrac{1+1+2+3+3+4+4+4+5}{9} = \dfrac{27}{9}$ (total sum of data) $= 3$ (number of pieces of data)

The MODE is the value that occurs most often.
For example, the mode of 1 1 2 3 3 **4 4 4** 5 is 4 as 4 occurs three times. 4 is the mode (or MODAL VALUE).

The MEDIAN is the value that is in the middle when the numbers are put in order.
For example, the median of 1 1 2 3 **3** 4 4 4 5 is 3.
(If the data are 1 2 3 **3 4** 4 4 5 the median would come halfway between 3 and 4. The median is then $\dfrac{3+4}{2} = \dfrac{7}{2} = 3.5$.

RANGE is the difference between the largest and the smallest number i.e. in **1** 1 2 3 3 4 4 4 **5** the range is 5 − 1 = 4.

• By putting the information in a frequency table (this one was also used on pages 102–103), you can find out averages more easily.

Number of Pets (x)	Frequency (f)	Total of Pets (fx)
0	8	8 x 0 = 0
1	12	12 x 1 = 12
2	5	5 x 2 = 10
3	3	3 x 3 = 9
4	2	2 x 4 = 8
Total	30	39

In this case the MEAN is $\dfrac{39}{30} = \dfrac{13}{10} = 1^3/_{10}$ i.e. more than 1 pet per child.

The MODE is 1 (12 pupils have 1 pet).

To find the MEDIAN, lay out the data as shown below:

0 0 0 0 0 0 0 0 1 1 1 1 1 1 **1 1** 1 1 1 1 2 2 2 2 2 3 3 3 4 4

The median is $\dfrac{1+1}{2} = 1$

The RANGE is 4 − 0 = 4 pets (the largest minus the smallest).

a) Find the MEAN of 18, 7, 12, 11, 32.   = ☐

b) In the end of term exams, John scored 520 in 8 subjects. Find his MEAN mark.   = ☐

c) Find the MODE of 10, 7, 11, 15, 10, 18, 12, 4, 10, 6.   = ☐

d) The heights (in centimetres) of 10 boys are 154, 155, 149, 153, 154, 148, 150, 154, 155, 152. What is their MODAL height?   = ☐

e) Find the MEDIAN of 4, 7, 12, 13, 16, 19, 21.   = ☐

f) What is the MEDIAN of 7, 3, 2, 4, 6, 8, 3, 4?   = ☐

g) Victoria scored the following marks in the Christmas tests: 72, 87, 77, 73, 86, 72, 69, 75. What is the RANGE of marks?   = ☐

h) In question (d), what is the RANGE of heights?   = ☐

In a test (out of 50) marks scored were:
43, 46, 47, 45, 45, 42, 47, 49, 43, 43.

i) Find the MEAN mark.   = ☐

j) Find the MODAL mark.   = ☐

k) Find the MEDIAN mark. = ☐

TEACHER'S TIP
Mean – Average
Median – Middle
Mode - Most

Probability predicts the likelihood of an event occurring. If an event is certain to occur, the probability is represented as a probability of 1.
• If an event is impossible and definitely will not occur its probability is represented by 0.
• The probability of any other events occurring between certainty and impossibility is represented by a fraction, a decimal or a percentage.

This is written using P to mean probability and placing the event that occurs in a bracket. E.g. P(x) ['x' stands for an event].

For example, where P = probability:

a) The probability that there will be daylight tomorrow is 1 (i.e. it is certain): P(daylight) = 1.

b) The probability that a triangle has 4 sides is 0 (i.e. it is impossible). P(triangle has 4 sides) = 0.

c) The probability that I will throw a 3 in one throw of a die in a board game is 1/6 (i.e. throwing a '3' is one of six possible outcomes). $P(3) = \dfrac{1}{6}$

d) The probability that I will NOT throw a 3 in one throw of a die in a board game is $1 - \dfrac{1}{6}$

i.e. $\dfrac{6}{6} - \dfrac{1}{6} = \dfrac{5}{6}$ or, $P = 1 - \dfrac{1}{6} = \dfrac{5}{6}$

This is certainty (1) of throwing a number MINUS the probability of throwing 3, $(\dfrac{1}{6})$.

To take another example:

At a bus stop, there are 15 people. 7 are men, 4 are women, 3 are boys and 1 is a girl.

A person is chosen at random. What is the probability that the person is a) a woman, b) male, c) female?

a) $P(\text{woman}) = \dfrac{4}{15}$

b) $P(\text{male}) = \dfrac{10}{15} = \dfrac{2}{3}$ (7 men + 3 boys = 10 males)

c) $P(\text{female}) = 1 - \dfrac{2}{3} = \dfrac{1}{3}$

i.e. Certainty − P(male)

TEST 55

Example If the probability of a rose flowering in November is 0.2, the probability of it not flowering in November is P(not flowering in November) = 1 – 0.2 = 0.8.

a) What is the probability that France is in Africa?   = ☐

b) What is the probability that a coin has two sides?   = ☐

c) What is the probability that a letter in the English alphabet is a vowel?   = ☐

d) What is the probability that a letter in the English alphabet is a consonant?   = ☐

e) What is the probability that a letter in the English alphabet is an 'm'?   = ☐

f) If a card is drawn from a pack of 52 cards, what is the probability that it is an ace?   = ☐

g) Emma has bought 5 raffle tickets. If a total of 1000 were sold, what is the probability that she will win?   = ☐

h) The probability that Charles will win a race is $\frac{2}{9}$. What is the probability that he will lose?   = ☐

i) The probability that it will be sunny on 11 November is 0.15. What is the probability that it will not be sunny? = ☐

j) In a raffle the probability of buying a winning ticket is $\frac{3}{146}$. What is the probability of buying a losing ticket? = ☐

k) A box contains red and yellow tulip bulbs. If the probability of choosing a red bulb is 0.65, what is the probability of choosing a yellow one?   = ☐

ANSWERS

NUMBERS AND ALGEBRA

TEST 1: a) 3 129 **b)** 33 204 **c)** 78 025 **d)** 60 202 **e)** 90 000 **f)** three thousand, seven hundred and twenty-one **g)** seventy-six thousand, two hundred and fourteen **h)** eighty thousand, one hundred and fifty seven **i)** sixty-seven thousand and two **j)** sixty thousand, one hundred **k)** 1 627 **l)** 35 355 **m)** 30 333 **n)** 73 373 **o)** 30 915 **p)** 21 111 **q)** 3 429 **r)** 38 320 **s)** 11 190

TEST 2: a) 3 260 **b)** 250 **c)** 423 700 **d)** 27 400 **e)** 27 000 **f)** 62 000 **g)** 9630 **h)** 3080 **i)** 69 300 **j)** 148 800 **k)** 513 000 **l)** 896 000

TEST 3: a) 23.6 **b)** 2.5 **c)** 7.24 **d)** 6.38 **e)** 2.734 **f)** 0.927 **g)** 2341 **h)** 2 106 r1 **i)** 822 r3 **j)** 3 211 r11 **k)** 1 333 r16 **l)** 413 r13 **m)** 488 r25 **n)** 864 r12

TEST 4: a) 5 082 **b)** 11 552 **c)** 3 174 **d)** 15 615 **e)** 17 376 **f)** 17 208 **g)** 22896 **h)** 33856 **i)** 26286 **j)** 40315 **k)** 26418 **l)** 60075

TEST 5: a) 242 r5 **b)** 1298 r31 **c)** 347 r5 **d)** 169 r 18 **e)** 558 r23 **f)** 1 253 r22 **g)** 674 r13 **h)** 674 r69 **i)** 333 r9 **j)** 524 r3 **k)** 627 r11 **l)** 504 r8

TEST 6: a) 6 **b)** 12 **c)** 10 **d)** 12 **e)** 12 **f)** 21 **g)** 20 **h)** 20 **i)** 5 **j)** 4 **k)** 3 **l)** 7 **m)** 4 **n)** 15 **o)** 4 **p)** 9 **q)** 3, 5, 7 **r)** 11, 13, 17, 19 **s)** 41, 43, 47, 53 **t)** 2 x 2 x 3 **u)** 7 x 5 **v)** 2 x 2 x 2 x 2 x 3 **w)** 2 x 2 x 3 x 5 **x)** 2 x 2 x 3 x 7 **y)** 2 x 2 x 2 x 2 x 3 x 3

TEST 7: a) > **b)** < **c)** < **d)** > **e)** -3, -2, 1 **f)** -3, -1, 1, 7 **g)** -5, -2, 3, 4 **h)** -3, -1, 5, 6 **i)** -5, -1, 4, 6 **j)** 10 **k)** 2 **l)** -2 **m)** -2 **n)** 4 **o)** -4 **p)** -2 **q)** 2 **r)** 24 **s)** -24 **t)** 21 **u)** -8 **v)** 15 **w)** 4 **x)** -4 **y)** 2 **z)** -4

TEST 8: a) 2^8 **b)** 7^5 **c)** 2^9 **d)** $8^4 \times 7^2$ **e)** 7^2 **f)** 6^2 **g)** 12^5 **h)** 9 **i)** 2^6 **j)** 9^{10} **k)** 7 **l)** 1 **m)** 19 **n)** 1 **o)** 8 **p)** 7 **q)** 3 **r)** 2 **s)** 4 and 5 **t)** 3 and 4 **u)** 5 and 6 **v)** 7 and 8 **w)** 1 **x)** 1

TEST 9: a) 10 **b)** 9 **c)** 12 **d)** 6 **e)** 24 **f)** 36 **g)** $^1/_4$ **h)** $^1/_4$ **i)** $^2/_3$ **j)** $^9/_{10}$ **k)** $^2/_5$ **l)** $^5/_7$ **m)** $2^5/_8$ **n)** $3^2/_5$ **o)** $4^1/_6$ **p)** $5^2/_3$ **q)** $5^3/_4$ **r)** $4^6/_7$ **s)** $^5/_2$ **t)** $^{25}/_4$ **u)** $^{17}/_3$ **v)** $^{35}/_8$ **w)** $^{71}/_8$ **x)** $^{52}/_5$ **y)** $^{43}/_{12}$ **z)** $^{71}/_9$

TEST 10: a) $^8/_9$ **b)** $1^1/_{15}$ **c)** $1^1/_8$ **d)** $^{17}/_{18}$ **e)** $2^1/_6$ **f)** $5^{13}/_{14}$ **g)** $10^{23}/_{24}$ **h)** $8^{29}/_{36}$ **i)** $^3/_8$ **j)** $^5/_{12}$ **k)** $^1/_8$ **l)** $^2/_{33}$ **m)** $^2/_{15}$ **n)** $1^9/_{20}$ **o)** $1^5/_6$ **p)** $2^{13}/_{24}$ **q)** $2^{26}/_{33}$

TEST 11: a) $^3/_{14}$ **b)** $^{10}/_{24} = ^5/_{12}$ **c)** $^{12}/_{45} = ^4/_{15}$ **d)** $^2/_6 = ^1/_3$ **e)** $^{12}/_{51} = ^4/_{17}$ **f)** $^1/_4$ **g)** $2^2/_3$ **h)** $1^4/_5$ **i)** $2^7/_8$ **j)** 12 **k)** $1^1/_4$ **l)** 30 **m)** $^1/_8$ **n)** $^1/_{12}$ **o)** $^2/_3$ **p)** 6 **q)** $1^5/_9$ **r)** $^{10}/_{27}$ **s)** $^1/_4$ **t)** $1^3/_7$ **u)** $3^3/_4$ **v)** $6^9/_{20}$ **w)** $16^1/_3$ **x)** $1^2/_{13}$

TEST 12: a) 267.158 **b)** 16 125.024 **c)** 7 800.175 **d)** 18.069 **e)** 12.27 **f)** Twenty-four point two five **g)** three hundred and twenty-seven point two four seven **h)** two thousand, one hundred and twenty point zero one seven **i)** 44.429 **j)** 636.126 **k)** 7674.4904
l) 553.42 **m)** 285.371 **n)** 2766.656 **o)** 0.37 **p)** 202.11 **q)** 301.75 **r)** 10.849 **s)** 169.885
t) 88.902

TEST 13: a) 1072.3 **b)** 6342.1 **c)** 7200.24 **d)** 2813.7 **e)** 1.3 **f)** 0.02 **g)** 33 **h)** 5.72
i) 223.52 **j)** 362.4 **k)** 65.76 **l)** 2405.2 **m)** 20.64 **n)** 1.6285 **o)** 2.967 **p)** 0.863 **q)** 0.0278
r) 0.0027 **s)** 458 **t)** 33655 **u)** 1234.4 **v)** 55.6 **w)** 45.36 **x)** 741.36

TEST 14: a) $\frac{1}{2}$ **b)** $\frac{7}{20}$ **c)** $\frac{7}{40}$ **d)** $\frac{1}{4}$ **e)** $\frac{3}{4}$ **f)** $\frac{2}{5}$ **g)** $1\frac{1}{3}$ **h)** $6\frac{79}{100}$ **i)** $198\frac{17}{1000}$
j) 0.5 **k)** 0.75 **l)** 0.625 **m)** 0.6 **n)** 0.428571 **o)** 0.4 **p)** 0.6 **q)** 0.17 **r)** 0.83
s) 0.711, 0.401, 0.246 **t)** 0.348, 0.248, 0.246 **u)** 1.2, 0.21, 0.12 **v)** 7.81, 7.801, 7.8 **w)** 3.4, 3.04, 3.004 **x)** 6.51, 6.505, 6.5

TEST 15: a) (i) 2.874 **(ii)** 2.87 **(iii)** 2.9 **b) (i)** 67.256 **(ii)** 67.26 **(iii)** 67.3 **c) (i)** 20.091
(ii) 20.09 **(iii)** 20.1 **d) (i)** 254.154 **(ii)** 254.15 **(iii)** 254.2 **e) (i)** 0.009 **(ii)** 0.01 **(iii)** 0.0
f) (i) 0.001 **(ii)** 0.00 **(iii)** 0.0 **g) (i)** 3.28 **(ii)** 3.3 **(iii)** 3 **h) (i)** 7.31 **(ii)** 7.3 **(iii)** 7
i) (i) 68.01 **(ii)** 68 **(iii)** 70 **j) (i)** 254 **(ii)** 250 **(iii)** 300 **k) (i)** 1250 **(ii)** 1300 **(iii)** 1000
l) (i) 2100 **(ii)** 2090 **(iii)** 2000 **m)** 14000 (700 x 20) **n)** 36000 (900 x 40)
o) 4 **p)** 8

TEST 16: a) 9/20 **b)** 1/20 **c)** 3/20 **d)** 2/5 **e)** 11/25 **f)** 16/25 **g)** 75% **h)** 27%
i) 9% **j)** 125% **k)** 12.5% **l)** 7.5% **m) (i)** 3/25 **(ii)** 0.12 **n) (i)** 3/10 **(ii)** 0.3 **o) (i)** 2/25
(ii) 0.08 **p)** 50% **q)** 30% **r)** 65% **s)** 140% **t)** 84% **u)** 87.5%

v)

Fraction	Percentage	Decimal
$\frac{3}{4}$	75%	0.75
$\frac{3}{5}$	**60%**	0.6
$\frac{11}{20}$	55%	**0.55**
$\frac{4}{5}$	80%	0.8
$\frac{3}{10}$	30%	**0.3**

TEST 17: a) 20% **b)** 20% **c)** 60% **d)** 43.3% **e)** 28.4% **f)** 40% **g)** 30% **h)** 25%
i) 41.6% **j)** 36 **k)** 128 **l)** 91p **m)** 47.25l **n)** 40.8m **o)** 216g **p)** 28% **q)** 12 **r)** 147

TEST 18: a) 234 **b)** 166 **c)** 108lb **d)** £312 **e)** £7920 **f)** 30% **g)** £33.60 **h)** £22.95
i) 20% **j)** £1085

TEST 19: a) 7x **b)** 9a **c)** 2m + 3n **d)** 11f + 5g **e)** 4y + 5x **f)** 6a + 2b **g)** 8 **h)** 5
i) 20 **j)** 18 **k)** 30 **l)** 28 **m)** 3a + 3b **n)** 6 − 2y **o)** 8b − 20 **p)** 2xy + 4x **q)** −27c − 6
r) -2p + 8 **s)** $xy - x^2$ **t)** y^4 **u)** a^9 **v)** $3a^2 + 5a$ **w)** $b^3 + b^2 + 5b$ **x)** $3c^2 + 3c$
y) $a^2 + 3b^2 + 3b$ **z)** $2m^2 + 3n^3 + n^2$

TEST 20: a) n = 2 **b)** p = 5 **c)** q = 3 **d)** r = 9 **e)** s = 2 **f)** t = 2 **g)** u = 1
h) v = 1 **i)** w = 3 **j)** x = 3

ANSWERS

TEST 21: a) y = 3 **b)** z = -2 **c)** a = 3 **d)** b = 3 **e)** b = 9 **f)** c = 14 **g)** d = 0
h) e = 3 $^3/_5$ **i)** f = -8 **j)** x = 10 **k)** g = $^1/_3$

TEST 22: a) v = 1 **b)** c = -12 **c)** a = 7 **d)** w = 1/4 **e)** p = 2 **f)** r = 2/5
g) 20 – (2s + 3t) **h)** c = £49x **i)** c = (27e + 19f) pence

TEST 23: a) $b = 1 - \dfrac{a}{x}$ **b)** $b = \dfrac{9a^2c}{6ac} = \dfrac{3a}{2}$ **c)** $\dfrac{y + z}{3} = w$ **d)** $\dfrac{3g}{2} = f$

e) $a = \dfrac{9}{(x + 2y + 3z)}$ **f)** y = 3c   **g)** $\dfrac{a - c}{2} = b$ **h)** 5(q – r) = p

i) v = -3u

TEST 24: a) 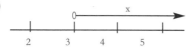   **b)**

c)    **d)**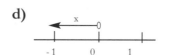

e) 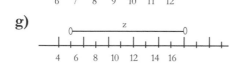   **f)**

g)

h) x – 3 < 9   **i)** x + 4 > 5
   x < 12   x > 1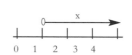

j) x – 5 < -3   **k)** x + 6 < 0
   x < -3 + 5    x < -6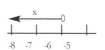
   x < 2

TEST 25: a) 12 : 4 :: 3 : 1 **b)** 7 : 35 :: 1 : 5 **c)** 12 : 15 :: 4 : 5 **d)** 27 : 6 :: 9 : 2
e) 20p : £1.04 :: 5 : 26 **f)** 20cm : 1m :: 1 : 5 **g)** 55ml : 1l :: 11 : 200 **h)** 10in : 8ft :: 5 : 48
i) 48g : 1kg :: 6 : 125 **j)** 260m : 1.5km :: 13 : 75

k) 4 : 18 :: x : 12 x = $\dfrac{48}{18}$ = $2\dfrac{2}{3}$ hours = 2 hours, 40 minutes

l) 156 : 12 :: x : 7 x = $\dfrac{7 \times 156}{12}$ = £91   **m)** 5 : 560 :: 7 : x x = $\dfrac{7 \times 560}{5}$ = £784

n) 500 : 15 :: 900 : x   x = $\dfrac{15 \times 900}{500}$ = £27

o) 900 : 12 :: 3300 : x x = $\dfrac{12 \times 3300}{900}$ = 44cm

TEST 26: a) 50, 60 **b)** 9, 6 **c)** 5, 2 **d)** 32, 64 **e)** 15, 21 **f)** 25, 36 **g)** 22, 15 **h)** 20, 25 **i)** 13, 15 **j)** 26, 30 **k)** 9, 4.5 **l)** 10000, 100000 **m)** $^1/_6$, $^1/_7$ **n)** 0.0001, 0.00001 **o)** -8, -10 **p)** 2, 5 **q)** 128, 256 **r)** 8, 4 **s)** 88, 77 **t)** 84, 96 **u)** 29, 35 **v)** 4, 8 **w)** 6.25, 3.125 **x)** $^1/_{16}$, $^1/_{32}$

TEST 27:

	1st	2nd	3rd	4th
a)	2	3	4	5
b)	2	4	6	8
c)	3	6	9	12
d)	5	6	7	8
e)	1	3	5	7
f)	0	5	10	15
g)	1	5	9	13
h)	10	8	6	4

i)

	1st	2nd	3rd	4th
	1 __3__ 4 __3__ 7 __3__ 10			
	3	6	9	12

Formula is 3n − 2

j)

	1st	2nd	3rd	4th
	8 __5__ 13 __5__ 18 __5__ 23			
	5	10	15	20

Formula is 5n + 3

k)

5 __6__ 11 __6__ 17 __6__ 23

6   12   18   24

Formula is 6n − 1

l)

4 __3__ 7 __3__ 10 __3__ 13

3   6   9   12

Formula is 3n + 1

TEST 28: a)

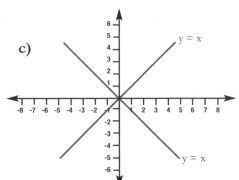

b)

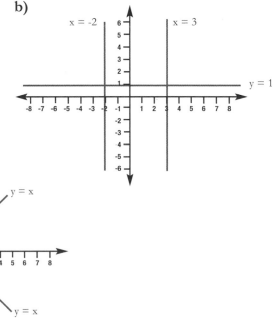

c)

ANSWERS

TEST 29:

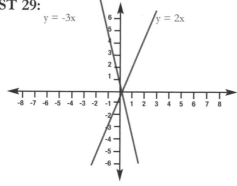

a) 6 **b)** -4 **c)** 0 **d)** -3 **e)** 3 **f)** 6 **g)** 0

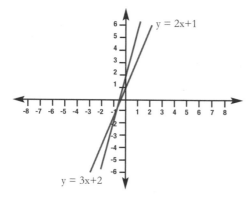

$y = 2x + 1$

h)

x	-2	0	2
y	-3	1	5

i) $y = 1$ **j)** 2 **k)** $y = 2x$, or, $y = 2x + 2$, or, $y = 2x + 3$ etc

l)

$y = 3x + 2$

x	-1	0	1
y	-1	2	5

m) $y = 2$ **n)** 3 **o)** $y = 3x$, or, $y = 3x + 1$, or, $y = 3x + 3$ etc

TEST 30:

a)

$y = 5 - 2x$

x	2	0	-2
y	1	5	7

$y = 3 - x$

x	2	0	-2
y	1	3	5

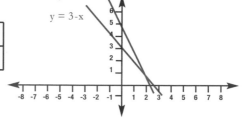

Solution $x = 2$, $y = 1$

120

b)

$$3x - y = 9$$
$$\underline{2x - y = 2}$$
$$x = 7$$

Substitute in 2

	$2x - y$	$= 2$
	$14 - y$	$= 2$
	12	$= y$
(test in 1:	$21 - 12$	$= 9)$
Therefore	x	$= 7, y = 12$

c)

$$2x + 2y = 14$$
$$\underline{2x + y = 9}$$
$$y = 5$$

Substitute in 2

	$2x + y$	$= 9$
	$2x + 5$	$= 9$
	$2x$	$= 9 - 5$
	$2x$	$= 4$
	x	$= 2$
(test in 1:	$4 + 10$	$= 14)$
Therefore	x	$= 2, y = 5$

d)

$$7x - y = 5$$
$$\underline{3x - y = 1}$$
$$4x = 4$$
$$x = 1$$

Substitute in 2

	$3x - y$	$= 1$
	$3 - y$	$= 1$
	$3 - 1$	$= y$
	2	$= y$
(test in 1:	$7 - 2$	$= 5)$
Therefore	x	$= 1, y = 2$

TEST 31· a) (i) 2 hours **(ii)** 45km/h **b) (i)** 8 hours **(ii)** 25mph **c) (i)** 4 hours **(ii)** 25mph **d) (i)** 4 hours **(ii)** 25km/h

e)

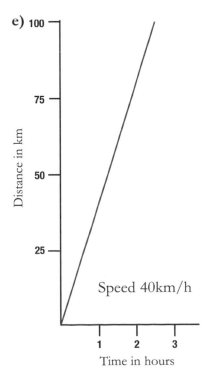

Speed 40km/h

f)

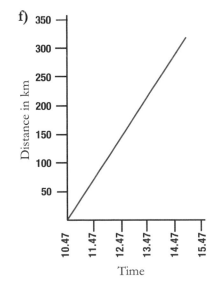

Speed 70mph

TEST 32: a) $x^2 + x = 50$

Try 6	$x^2 + x = 36 + 6 = 42$	too small
Try 7	$x^2 + x = 49 + 7 = 56$	too big
Try 6.5	$x^2 + x = 42.25 + 6.5 = 48.75$	too small
Try 6.6	$x^2 + x = 43.56 + 6.5 = 50.16$	too big
Try 6.55	$x^2 + x = 42.9025 + 6.55 = 49.4525$	too small, but very close

Solution is x = 6.6 to 1 decimal place

b) $x^3 - x = 50$

Try 4	$x^3 - x = 64 - 4 = 60$	too big
Try 3	$x^3 - x = 27 - 3 = 24$	too small
Try 3.6	$x^3 - x = 46.656 - 3.6 = 43.056$	too small
Try 3.7	$x^3 - x = 50.653 - 3.7 = 46.953$	too small
Try 3.8	$x^3 - x = 54.872 - 3.8 = 51.072$	too big
Try 3.75	$x^3 - x = 52.734 - 3.75 = 48.984$	too small, but very close

Solution is x = 3.8 to 1 decimal place

c) $x + \frac{1}{x} = 7$

Try 6	$x + \frac{1}{x} = 6 + 0.166 = 6.166$	too small
Try 6.5	$x + \frac{1}{x} = 6.5 + 0.154 = 6.654$	too small
Try 6.8	$x + \frac{1}{x} = 6.8 + 0.147 = 6.947$	too small
Try 6.9	$x + \frac{1}{x} = 6.9 + 0.145 = 7.045$	too big, but very close

Solution is x = 6.9 to 1 decimal place

d) $x^4 = 14$

Try 2	$x^4 = 16$	too big
Try 1.5	$x^4 = 5.0625$	too small
Try 1.8	$x^4 = 10.498$	too small
Try 1.9	$x^4 = 13.0321$	too small, but very close

Solution is x = 1.9 to 1 decimal place

e) $x^2 = 7x$ Therefore $x^2 - 7x = 0$

Try x = 7 $x^2 - 7x = 49 - 49 = 0$

Solution is x = 7

SPACE, SHAPE AND MEASURES

TEST 33: a) $180°$ **b)** $90°$ **c)** obtuse **d)** $50°$ **e)** $130°$ **f)** $60°$ **g)** $30°$ **h)** $150°$ **i)** $30°$
j) $120°$ **k)** $30°$ **l)** (example)

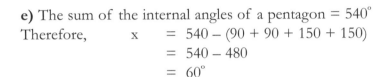

TEST 34: a) (i) $40°$ (ii) $100°$ **b)** $50°$ **c)** (i) $150°$ (ii) $80°$ (iii) $70°$ **d)** Yes, SAS
e) (i) $i = 40°$ (ii) $j = 140°$ (iii) $k = 40°$ (iv) $l = 40°$ (v) $m = 40°$ (vi) $n = 100°$ (vii) $o = 40°$

TEST 35: a) 4 **b)** 0 **c)** 4 **d)** $16cm^2$ **e)** $35cm^2$ **f)** $17 \times 8 = 136cm^2$ **g)** $70cm^2$
h) $24 + 4 = 28cm^2$

TEST 36: a) $(5 \times 180°) - 360° = 540°$ **b)** $540/5 = 108°$ **c)**

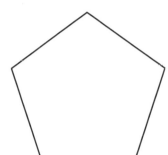

d) $\dfrac{180 (12 - 2)}{12} = \dfrac{1800}{12} = 150°$

e) The sum of the internal angles of a pentagon $= 540°$
Therefore, $\qquad x \quad = 540 - (90 + 90 + 150 + 150)$
$\qquad\qquad\qquad\quad = 540 - 480$
$\qquad\qquad\qquad\quad = 60°$

f) $360/8 = 45°$

TEST 37: a) 10m **b)** 5m **c)** 40cm **d)** 8cm **e)** 12in **f)** 26m

TEST 38: a) 6.3cm **b)** 11.3mm **c)** 9.4in **d)** 12.6cm **e)** 4.1m **f)** 7.5in

TEST 39: a) 1 PS
         2 PQ
         3 QR
         4 SR
         5 POR – Diameter

b)

d) $C = 2\pi r$
$\qquad = 2 \times 3.142 \times 4$
$\qquad = 25.136cm$

e) $= \pi r^2$
$\qquad = 3.142 \times 3 \times 3$
$\qquad = 3.142 \times 9$
$\qquad = 28.278cm^2$

f) $C = \pi d$
$\qquad = 3.142 \times 5$
$\qquad = 15.710 \text{ cm}$

ANSWERS

TEST 40: a) 576cm³ **b)** 0.12m³

c) (i)   (iii)

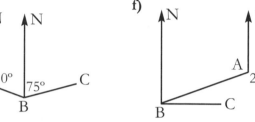

(ii)

d) (i)   (iii)

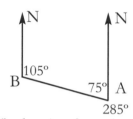

(ii)

TEST 41: a) 065° **b)** 120° **c)** 260° **d)** 295°

e)

N   N

A $\overset{110°}{}$ $\overset{75°}{}$ C

B

f)

N   N

A 250°

B   C

g)

N   N

B $\overset{105°}{}$ 75° A

285°

The bearing from A to B is 105°

TEST 42: a) Translation $\binom{4}{3}$ **b)** Translation $\binom{4}{4}$ **c)** Reflection on the y axis

d) Translation $\binom{-6}{-3}$ **e)**

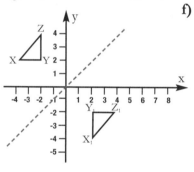

f)

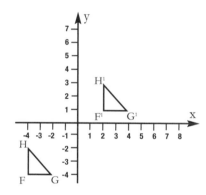

TEST 43: a) ABC is rotated 90° clockwise through (1, 0) **b)** ABC is rotated 180° through (1, 0)
c) ABC is rotated 180° through A (1, 0)

TEST 44: a)

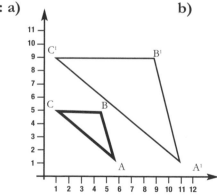

b)

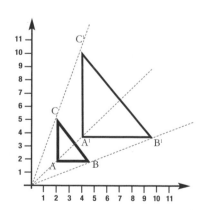

c) (i) Enlargement scale factor 2, centre (0, 0) **(ii)** Rotation 180° clockwise through (0, 0)

124

TEST 45: a) 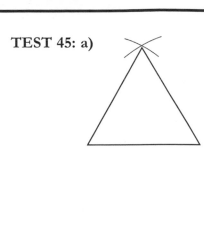   **b)** 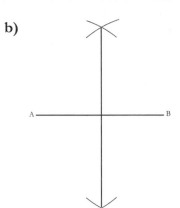   **c)**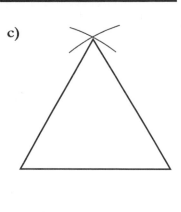

TEST 46: a) 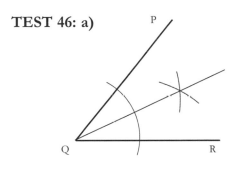   **b)** 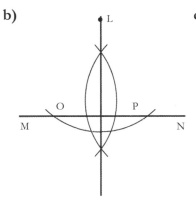   **c)**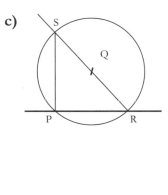

TEST 47: a) 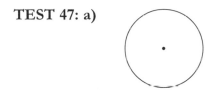   **b)**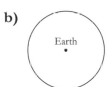

c)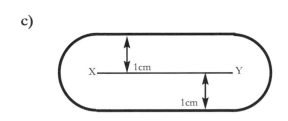

ANSWERS

HANDLING DATA

TEST 48: (SAMPLE QUESTIONNAIRE)

a) 1 Do you eat breakfast? Yes ☐ No ☐

2 How long do you take to eat breakfast at the weekend?
5 minutes ☐   10 minutes ☐
15 minutes ☐   20 minutes ☐
20+ minutes ☐

3 How long do you have for breakfast midweek?
5 minutes ☐   10 minutes ☐
15 minutes ☐   20 minutes ☐
20+ minutes ☐

b) 1 How do you come to school?
By foot ☐   By bike ☐
By car ☐   By bus ☐
By train ☐   By bus and train ☐
By other means ☐

c) 1 Do you receive pocket money? Yes ☐ No ☐

2 Do you earn money? Yes ☐ No ☐

3 How much do you spend on yourself weekly?
£0–5 ☐   £6–10 ☐   £10+ ☐

4 Would you spend it in shops or mail order?
Shops ☐   Mail Order ☐

5 Which goods do you buy most often with your own money?
Food and drink ☐   Sweets ☐   Magazines ☐
Make-up ☐   Clothes ☐ Sports goods ☐
Stationery ☐   CDs ☐   Computer games ☐

TEST 49:

a)

Shoe size	Tally	Frequency
2	IIII I	5
3	IIII I I	6
4	IIII I I	6
5	IIII I	5
6	II	2
	Total	24

b)

Weight	Tally	Frequency
0–1	IIII I II	7
2–3	IIII I III	8
4–5	IIII I IIII I II	12
6	III	3
	Total	30

c)

Ages	Tally	Frequency
16 < a < 25	IIII I IIII I	10
26 < a < 35	IIII I IIII I	10
36 < a < 45	IIII	4
46 < a < 55	IIII I IIII	9
56 < a < 65	IIII I II	7
	Total	40

TEST 50: a)

(i)

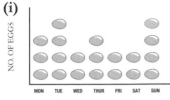

(ii)

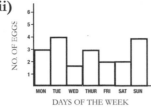

(iii)

b)

(i)

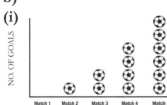

(ii)

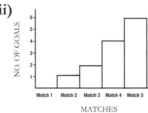

(iii)

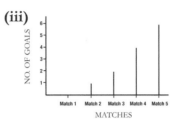

TEST 51: a)

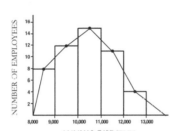

b)

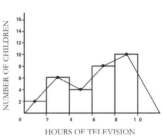

c)

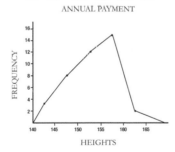

d)

0	9				
10	1	2			
20	0	4	8		
30	2	3	4	6	
40	0	2	5	5	7	8

TEST 52:

a)

36 pupils	$360/36 = 10°$	Therefore $10°$ represents 1 pupil
7 pupils –	70°	**BLACK**
12 pupils –	120°	**FAIR**
1 pupil –	10°	**BLOND**
8 pupils –	80°	**BROWN**
2 pupils –	20°	**RED**
6 pupils –	60°	**AUBURN**
Total	360°	

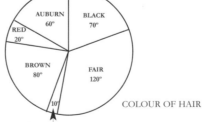

ANSWERS

b)   60 trees $360/_{60} = 6°$ Therefore 6° represents 1 tree

          20 trees –   120° **LIME**
          10 trees –   60° **SYCAMORE**
          9 trees –   54° **HORSE CH.**
          5 trees –   30° **BEECH**
          8 trees –   48° **BIRCH**
          6 trees –   36° **OAK**
          2 trees –   12° **MAPLE**
          Total   360°

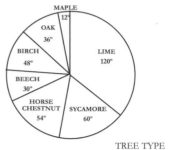

TREE TYPE

c)   British   = 90°/360 x 1080   = 270
       French   = 70° x 3   = 210
       German = 80° x 3   = 240
       Spanish = 70° x 3   = 210
       Italian   = 50° x 3   = <u>150</u>

       Total   <u>1080</u>

TEST 53: a)

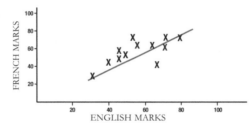

Strong positive correlation

b)

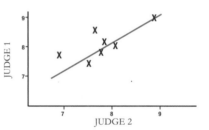

Strong positive correlation

c)

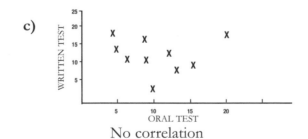

No correlation

TEST 54: a) 16   **b)** 65   **c)** 10   **d)** 154   **e)** 13   **f)** 2, 3, 3, 4, 4, 6, 7, 8 – Median is 4
g) 87 – 69 = 18   **h)** 155 – 148 = 7cm   **i)** $450/_{10} = 45$ **j)** 43
k) 42, 43, 43, 43, 45, – 45, 46, 47, 47, 49 – Median mark is 45

TEST 55: a) 0   **b)** 1   **c)** $5/_{26}$ **d)** $21/_{26}$ **e)** $1/_{26}$ **f)** $4/_{52} = 1/_{13}$ **g)** $5/_{1000} = 1/_{200}$
h) $1 – 2/_{9} = 7/_{9}$ **i)** 1 – 0.15 = 0.85   **j)** $1 – 3/_{146} = 143/_{146}$ **k)** 1 – 0.65 = 0.35